The *Tourist*
TRAVEL AND FIELD GUIDE OF THE
Serengeti
NATIONAL PARK

Written by
Veronica Roodt
Published by Papyrus Publications
2005

Published by Papyrus Publications

PO Box 367
Hartebeespoort
0216
Republic of South Africa

First published in 2005

Written by Veronica Roodt
Printed by: House of Print: Tel (+27) (11) 493-8516 (Johannesburg, South Africa)

Photographs: All photographs and illustrations by Veronica Roodt except where
otherwise indicated.

Distributed by:
Veronica Roodt - Papyrus Publications
    Tel/Fax: (+27) (12) 253-2883 (Pretoria, South Africa)
    Email: vericon@mweb.co.za
    Website: www.veronicaroodt.co.za
Veronica Roodt Distributors
    Tel/Fax: (+27) (12) 549-1355 (Pretoria, South Africa)
    Email: veronicaroodt@lantic.net

In order to improve and update the book and maps, feedback is welcome. Please
contact Veronica Roodt at address: PO Box 365, Hartebeespoort, 0216, South
Africa or email: vericon@mweb.co.za or tel/fax: (+27) (12) 253-2883, Pretoria,
South Africa.

ISBN 0-620-34190-4

PREFACE

The aim of any map, travel guide or field guide book is to improve the tourist's experience by offering concise, accurate and easy-to-use information. Weight and space restrictions often limit the number of books one can carry. It thus makes sense to combine detailed maps, travel information and a photographic field guide into one publication. This book consists of the following:

- A map of the Serengeti National Park plus 9 detailed satellite maps of all tourist areas.
- The first section consists of a travel guide with information on how to get there, where to stay, road conditions, best season to visit and climate. It also includes detailed maps and background information on the history, people, topography, geology and archaeology.
- The second part consists of a field guide that includes check lists and over 500 photographs of the plants, mammals, birds, reptiles and amphibians one is most likely to see. The text provides information on the nutritional value and medicinal uses of plants, habitat preferences of large mammals as well as interesting animal and bird behaviour.
- A comprehensive index for easy reference is at the back of the book.

The main objective of this book is to promote this incredible part of Africa, to stimulate an interest in nature and inspire more and more people to visit the Serengeti National Park - one of the last true natural treasures left on earth.
Enjoy your visit!

ACKNOWLEDGMENTS

I want to thank the Tanzania National Parks for affording me the opportunity to work in the Serengeti National Park. In particular, I would like to thank Mr JM Kessy for his kind and friendly assistance throughout the project. Without him, none of this would be possible. I also want to thank the Chief Park Warden of the Serengeti National Park, Mr Handu, the tourism staff and the ecology staff for their assistance during the field work of the map, specifically Eunice Msangi, Nelson Joseph, Ernest Sitta and Dora Aroyce who were very kind and helpful. Then I want to thank the Frankfurt Zoological Society for supplying me with information regarding the Serengeti National Park and for their assistance in general. My appreciation to Monument Toyota, Constantia for their generous contribution in partly sponsoring my vehicle.

A very sincere thanks to my assistant, Lenyatso July, who accompanied me on all the trips to Tanzania and who assisted with the tracking of the roads. His input was vital to the project. I also want to thank Pieter Swart for his help with the maps and Rob Kauzil for his invaluable help with the editing. Most importantly, my sincerest appreciation to Janine Fourie for her motivation, assistance and patience throughout the project.

Veronica Roodt

ABBREVIATIONS

Abbreviations used throughout the book:		NCA	-	Ngorongoro Conservation Area
SNP	- Serengeti National Park	NCAA	-	Ngorongoro Conservation Area Authority
TANAPA	- Tanzania National Parks	FZS	-	Frankfurt Zoological Society

CONTENTS

MAP REFERENCES

MAP REFERENCES

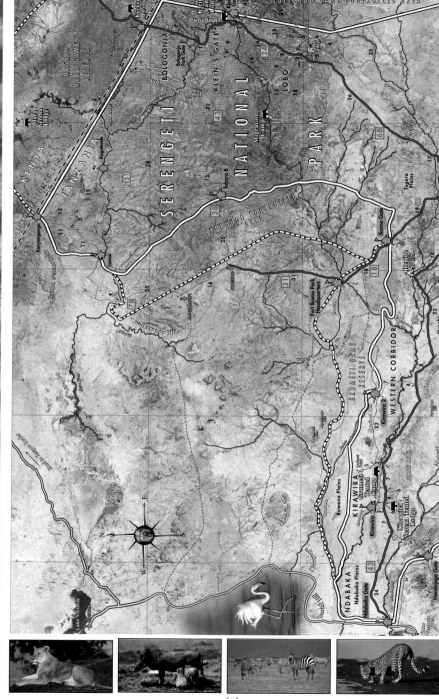

SERENGETI NATIONAL PARK

MAP 1

The Tourist Map of the Serengeti National Park

Hippopotamus

INTRODUCTION

Rongai area north of Moru Kopjes in the Serengeti National Park

The mere mention of the name 'Serengeti' conjures up images of vast open plains, dotted with flat-topped *Acacia* Trees and brimming with wildlife, of Lions scouting the horizon from the comfort of a rocky vantage point, of Hyenas squabbling at a carcass and of Vultures soaring high above.

The original Maasai meaning of the word 'Siringet' - 'the place where the land goes on forever' - probably only truly comes to life from the Vulture's vantage point. Imagine having a bird's-eye view of this vast stretch of land - the stage for the most dramatic wildlife interactions imaginable. A unique aspect of the Serengeti is that the stage shifts with the seasons in a clockwise rotational system as animals migrate. However, the main players remain the same - the migratory ungulates, predators and scavengers.

As conditions become harsher with the approaching dry season, both the hunters and the hunted become more desperate in their struggle to survive. The desperation of the ungulates culminates in the death-defying crossing of the crocodile-infested waters of the Grumeti and the Mara Rivers on their route north, where hundreds, maybe thousands of animals succumb to crocodiles, trampling and drowning.

The predators that remain on the plains also have to overcome the difficulties of finding food and water in a landscape that becomes increasingly scorched and inhospitable as the pans dry up, shimmering in the heat and almost devoid of any life.

But then the early rains bring welcome relief as the first trickles of the migratory herds arrive on the plains, shortly after which the bulk of the migration descends in its millions. Here they bear their young and take advantage of the temporary pans and the nutritious short grasses of the plains - only to repeat the cycle again and again, as they have done for over a million years.

Today, this migratory herd of animals is the largest left on earth and they move freely within the Serengeti Ecosystem, even across international borders. The awe-inspiring natural phenomenon of the migration certainly contributes to the fame of the Serengeti, but there is much more to this wonderful place - hills, valleys, lakes, rivers that feed Lake Victoria (the source of the Nile) and a staggering variety and number of wild creatures. Today, the Serengeti is probably the most famous national park in the world.

Hopefully this book will inspire more people to visit the Serengeti and be witness to the fact that the famous book and film by the Grzimeks, *Serengeti Shall Not Die*, which was produced almost 50 years ago, was only the beginning of an enormous effort to save this incredible place and the wildlife it supports. Thanks to the continued efforts, committment and dedication of the Tanzanian Government, Tanzania National Parks, the Frankfurt Zoological Society, researchers, scientists and the people of Tanzania, it can proudly be said that the 'Serengeti Did Not Die'!

The vast plains of the Serengeti

The SNP is situated on a high plateau in northern Tanzania, directly east of Lake Victoria, south-east of the Isuria Escarpment and west of the Gregory Rift Valley and the Ngorongoro highlands. All the above form the physical boundaries of a functioning ecosystem, in the centre of which the Serengeti is safely

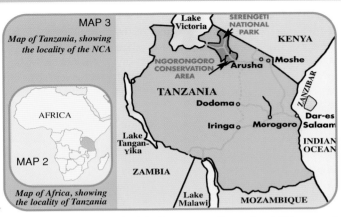

MAP 3

Map of Tanzania, showing the locality of the NCA

MAP 2

Map of Africa, showing the locality of Tanzania

nestled between wildlife buffer zones, as shown on the map below. It lies between 1°20′ and 3°20′ South and 33°50′ and 36°00′ East. The western corridor reaches almost up to Lake Victoria and there are plans to extend it up to the lake.

Naabi Entrance Gate is 290km and Seronera is 320km west of Arusha. Naabi Gate is 78km from the Ngorongoro Crater. The road is tarred from Arusha up to Ngorongoro entrance gate (Lodoare Gate) and gravelled for the rest of the way.

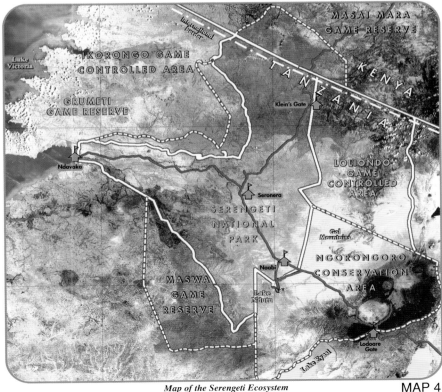

Map of the Serengeti Ecosystem

MAP 4

Size and elevation

Size The SNP covers an area of 14 763km². It forms the central and largest part of the Serengeti Ecosystem, which consists of the following components:

Masai Mara Game Reserve	1 672km²
Serengeti National Park	14 763km²
Ngorongoro Conservation Area	8 288km²
Grumeti Game Controlled Area	416km²
Ikorongo Game Reserve	563km²
Maswa Game Reserve	2 200km²
Loliondo Game Controlled Area	not sure

The whole ecosystem comprises an area of about 30 000km² (see map on pg 3).

Elevation The Serengeti National Park occupies a part of the high plateau in which the Serengeti Ecosystem is situated. It varies in elevation from 920m near the shores of Lake Victoria to 1 850m in the east. It lies much lower than the Ngorongoro Crater highlands which are 3 600m above sea level at their highest point.

Access to the Serengeti National Park

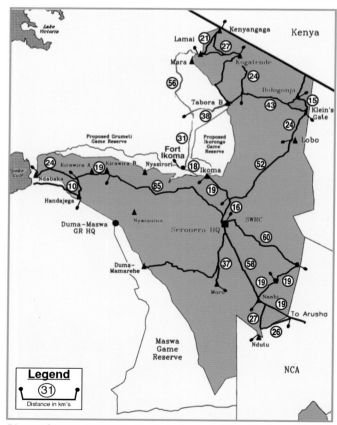

By air All the major tourist areas in the Serengeti, like Seronera, Ndutu, Moru, Kirawira and Lobo, have airstrips.

By road The main entrance gates to the park are at Naabi Gate in the south, Handajega and Ndabaka Gates in the west, Ikoma Gate north of Seronera and Klein's Gate in the north near Lobo. Special permission is required to travel from the Serengeti to the Masai Mara Game Reserve in Kenya via Bologonja Gate, where there is a customs and immigration post. However, this route is not generally used by the public. There are no tarred roads in the Serengeti but the main routes are gravelled.

Distances between main tourist areas in the Serengeti National Park **MAP 5**

The main distances between tourist areas are supplied below. Also refer to the map on the opposite page.

Seronera - Naabi Gate	58km	Naabi Gate - Lake Ndutu	27km
Seronera - Ndabaka Gate	128km	Naabi Gate - Gol Kopjes	19km
Seronera - Ikoma Gate	35km	Naabi Gate - Barafu Kopjes	38km
Seronera - Klein's Gate	92km	Naabi Gate - Ndabaka Gate	186km
Seronera - Moru Kopjes	37km	Naabi Gate - Ikoma Gate	93km
Seronera - Barafu Kopjes	60km	Naabi Gate - Klein's Gate	150km
Seronera - Lobo	68km	Naabi Gate - Bologonja	165km
Seronera - Bologonja	107km	Naabi Gate - Lobo	126km
Seronera - Lake Ndutu	85km	Naabi Gate Kenyanganga	219km
Seronera - Kenyanganga	161km	Naabi Gate - Seronera	58km

Climate

Rainfall The SNP falls into the bimodal rain pattern of East Africa, suggesting that there are two rainy seasons in the period from November to May. The short rains are from November to December and are brought on by the northern monsoon. The long rains are brought on by the south-eastern monsoon and last from February/March to May, with a short period of low rainfall or no rainfall during January and early February. Parts of the Serengeti, such as the Serengeti Plains and the Ndutu area, lie in the 'rain shadow' of the Ngorongoro highlands. The term 'rain-shadow' refers to the clouds coming in from the Indian Ocean in the east that 'break' against the Ngorongoro highlands, resulting in rain. The few clouds that manage to pass the highlands evaporate before they can supply rain. This area is thus very dry compared to other areas of the park. The annual rainfall varies from ±500mm in the south-east to ±1 200mm in the north-west.

Temperatures The temperature is relatively uniform throughout the year with maximum temperatures of around 28°C. The minimum temperature in May to August is about 13°C. Extreme heat and extreme cold is the exception rather than the rule in the Serengeti National Park.

A rainstorm building up in the Serengeti - a common sight during the rainy season

The headquarters of the Tanzanian National Parks are situated in Arusha. The Park headquarters are partly located at Seronera and partly at Fort Ikoma, which is 49km north-west of Seronera. There are four anti-poaching operational zones - at Kirawira, Duma, Lobo and Lamai - as well as twelve outposts and five gates. Tourism is administered from Seronera. The head of the Serengeti National Park is the Chief Park Warden, who resides at Seronera.

There is also a veterinary department, maintanence department and an ecology department. Ecology staff do monthly trips to all the outposts in the Serengeti to gather information on rainfall, temperatures, animal movements, etc. There is also a research institute at Seronera that co-ordinates many of the research projects. They have a good library, herbarium and other research facilities.

Ecology staff do monthly trips to all outposts to gather data

Maasai Giraffe

Pre-history

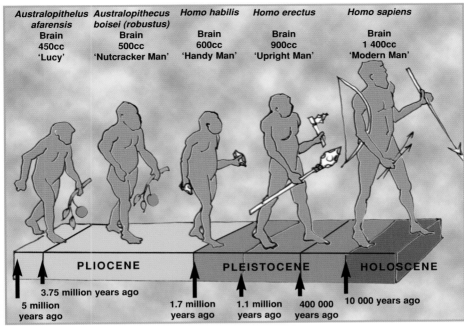

Australopithelus afarensis	Australopithecus boisei (robustus)	Homo habilis	Homo erectus	Homo sapiens
Brain 450cc 'Lucy'	Brain 500cc 'Nutcracker Man'	Brain 600cc 'Handy Man'	Brain 900cc 'Upright Man'	Brain 1 400cc 'Modern Man'

PLIOCENE — PLEISTOCENE — HOLOSCENE

3.75 million years ago
5 million years ago
1.7 million years ago
1.1 million years ago
400 000 years ago
10 000 years ago

The early hominids of the area

DISCOVERIES AT OLDUVAI GORGE

Although the pre-history of the area is based on evidence found in the Olduvai Gorge and at Laetoli in the Ngorongoro Conservation Area, it is representative of the archaeology of the entire area because of the close proximity. The Olduvai Gorge just provided a deep cut in the earth's crust, enabling us to see the evidence of early life within the layers.

The discovery of 'Zinj' Mary and Louis Leakey spent much of their adult life at Olduvai Gorge and made several discover-ies of human fossils, but their finds from 1930 to 1958 were mainly of animal fos-sils and stone tools.

Nutcracker Man or 'Zinj' (Australopithecus boisei)

Their great find was a fairly complete Australopithene-type skull found by Mary Leakey on 17 July 1959. It was a robust skull which they named *Zinjanthropus boisei*, later named *Australopithecus boisei*, also referred to as *A. robustus* or 'Zinj'. It is believed to have been robust, vegeterian with a small brain (500cc).

Discovery of *Homo habilis* It was at first suggested that Zinj had made the scrapers and tools found at Olduvai, but it is now thought that the stone tools were made by 'Handy Man' or *Homo habilis*, whose fossil remains also occur at Olduvai. *Homo habilis* made tools and probably hunted small animals. It was smaller than Zinj but it had a slightly larger brain of 600cc. It disappeared about 1,5 million years ago.

7

Discovery of *Australopithecus afarensis*

It was found that both the above hominids were descendants of *Australopithecus afarensis*, the best fossil remains of which were recovered in Ethiopia in 1974. Informally it became famous as 'Lucy', named after the Beatles' song *Lucy in the Sky with Diamonds*, which was a favourite camp song at the time.

The Laetoli Footprints were also found to have been made by *A. afarensis*. They were discovered in 1976 by Mary Leakey in an area called Laetoli, south of Olduvai Gorge and not too far north-west of Endulen in the Ngorongoro Conservation Area. *A. afarensis* was more ape-like than human and only ±1,3m tall but what distinguished them from other apes is that they walked on two legs. *A. afarensis* had a brain size of 450cc - about one third of the modern human brain. Bone evidence of it was also found at the Laetoli site. The Laetoli Footprints were dated at 3,75 million years old - well over a million years before the earliest evidence of stone tools appeared.

Discovery of *Homo erectus*

When *Homo habilis* disappeared about 1,5 million years ago, it made place for *Homo erectus* or 'Upright Man'. *Homo erectus* had a larger brain (900cc) and it had the ability to make better stone tools, such as axes.

History & people

The history of the people that inhabited the Serengeti is not as rich as that of the Ngorongoro highlands area, probably because of the presence of the Tsetse Fly, the host to a virus that causes disease in animals and man. However, there is evidence of early Watindiga (Hadzabe), Maasai and German occupation. The Maasai only left as recently as 1959.

Hadzabe or Watindiga tribe

The earliest known human inhabitants of the area were probably of the Hadzabe or Watindiga tribe, which today live near Lake Eyasi. They were not a warrior tribe but lived as hunter-gatherers, hunting by means of bows and poisoned arrows. The Hadzabe speak a click language, are of slight build with prominent, high cheekbones, of light skin and they smoke bone pipes. Interestingly, all the above characteristics correspond with that of the San (also known as Bushmen) of Botswana, Namibia, Angola and South Africa, ±5 000km to the south. Cultural sites indicative of their presence were found along the Mbalageti River in the western Serengeti.

The Maasai

About 200 years ago the Maasai moved into the Serengeti/ Ngorongoro area, probably in search of grazing for their cattle. As a fierce warrior tribe, many battles followed, mainly with the Datoga. The Maasai eventually secured the area but even today they speak of their ancient enemy with deference, referring to the Datoga as the Mang'ati, which means 'respected enemy'.

Maasai

From the late 1890s the Maasai were severely affected by Rinderpest, drought, famine and locusts. Legislation under colonial rule denied the Maasai much of their previous dry-season grazing. In 1958, twelve elders signed a treaty in which they relinquished their rights to graze their cattle in the Serengeti and about 1 000 Maasai, 23 000 cattle and 15 000 small stock were relocated to the Ngorongoro Conservation Area, where about 40 000 Maasai live today.

The Europeans During the period of colonisation, the Germans occupied Tanzania and called it Deutch Ost-Afrika. Historical sites of German occupation were found in the western corridor of the Serengeti. By the turn of the century hunters and explorers were well acquainted with the area. The first recorded European sighting of the Serengeti Plains was by the German explorer, Baumann. In March 1892 he saw the Ngorongoro Crater for the first time. After exploring the crater, he made his way to the west towards the Serengeti Plains. What he found was not a pleasant sight. A desperation hung over the area like a cloud - the result of the Rinderpest pandemic that ravaged through Africa and left millions of animals dead and people starving of hunger.

Hunting was rife early in the 1900s

Although animal numbers were not nearly what they are today, the Seronera area soon recovered, at least partly, after the Rinderpest. Word got out and in the early 1900s there was an influx of European hunters and collectors, like James Clarke and Stewart Edward White, soon followed. They reported 'animal numbers previously unheard of', encouraging more hunters to use the Seronera Valley as their hunting grounds. It became famous, not least for the large concentration of Lions. How sad to think that in those days the big cats were considered vermin and could be shot for pleasure. Accounts of safaris during the 1920s describe the killing of up to 50 Lions on a single trip! Rhinos were hunted for pleasure and left to rot most of the time. The ivory trade took its toll on the Elephant population. African Hunting Dogs were also considered vermin and were often killed on sight. In fact, this was the case in many African countries, including South Africa. The local tribes, who managed to live in complete harmony with the wild animals for centuries, stood helpless against the might of the rifle.

INTRODUCTION

Establishment of the Serengeti

During the early 1900s, it was soon realised that with continued exploitation, the game numbers would be completely decimated. The German colonists drew up legislation to protect wildlife in the area, but then World War I broke out and hunting continued.

After World War I the British took over the area and most Germans left. They called it 'Tanganyika Territory'. In 1921, the Game Conservation Ordinance was introduced by the British and in 1928 hunting and agriculture were prohibited in the Ngorongoro Crater.

In 1929 a 2 286km^2 area in the central part of the Serengeti - around the Seronera area - was declared a game reserve, but sport hunting was still allowed.

The Government started developing the area in the early 1930s. During this time a road was constructed from Karatu to Loliondo, the latter being the administrative centre of the area. Subsequently a road was built from Karatu to Mwanza, a town situated on the banks of Lake Victoria. The start of tourism was marked by the building of a log-cabin lodge on the rim of the Ngorongoro Crater. In 1935 the hunting of Lions in the Seronera Valley was prohibited.

In 1951 the Serengeti National Park was established which, at that time, included the area that we know today as the Ngorongoro Conservation Area. In 1957 Professor Bernard Grzimek and his son, Michael, started doing the first aerial counts of the animals of the Serengeti (see the box on pg 55 for more details). In 1959 the park was divided into the Serengeti National Park and the Ngorongoro Conservation Area. The Lamai Wedge, situated between the Mara River and the Kenya border, was added to the Serengeti National Park to compensate for the loss. All Maasai residents in the Serengeti were asked to move to the Ngorongoro Consevation Area. In 1981 the Serengeti National Park, together with the Ngorongoro Consevation Area, was declared an International Biosphere Reserve.

Buffalo with Red-billed Oxpecker

INTRODUCTION

TOPOGRAPHY, GEOLOGY & SOILS

Lobo Hills

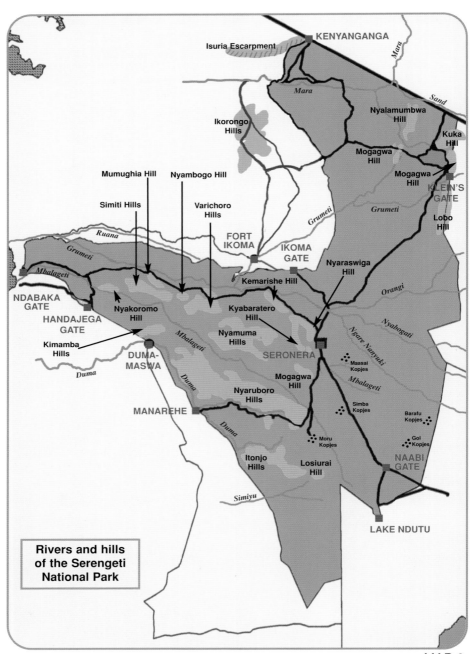

Main topographical features of the Serengeti National Park

MAP 6

Rivers and hills
of the Serengeti
National Park

MAJOR TOPOGRAPHICAL AREAS OF THE SNP

The Serengeti National Park consists not only of the plains, but also of hills, valleys and a number of rivers, many of which flow from east to west into Lake Victoria. The following are the major topographical areas:

Short Grass Plains in the south-east The southern and south-eastern sections of the park comprise the vast, open Short Grass Plains which are dotted with rocky outcrops or 'kopjes' (pronounced 'copies').

Undulating hills and open grassland in the south and west The south and west consist of undulating hills and of open grasslands. The woody vegetation consists mainly of thorny *Acacia* and *Commiphora* trees.

Tall grassland and woodland in the north and north-west The north and north-west is more undulating and the soil is more sandy. It also has a higher rainfall, resulting in dense, tall grassland and broad-leafed woodland vegetation.

THE HILLS

The north-western border The north-western section of the Serengeti is bordered by the Isuria Escarpment.

Northern part of the Serengeti The northern hills consist mainly of gneisses and granites as well as a few of metacherts and quartzite. North of the Bologonja River are the Nyalamumbwa, the Kuka and the Mogagwa Hills. South of the Bologonja River are the Lobo and the Ngalek Hills.

Western corridor In the western corridor are the Simiti, Mumaghia, Nyambogo and Varichoro Hills. The Simiti Hills consist of metacherts and jaspilite.

West of Seronera The underlying rocks west of Seronera consist of *Precambrian* volcanic rocks and banded ironstone of the Tanganyika shield, estimated at 2 500 million years old. West of Seronera are the Nyaraswiga, the Kerimishi and the Mukoma Hills. The Kerimishi Hills, however, consist of sandstone, quartzite and shale.

South-west In the south-west are the Nyamuma, Nyaruburo and the Itonjo Hills. The Nyaruboro and Itonjo Hills consist of sandstone, quartzite and shale and the Nyamuma Hills of granite.

Hills east of Seronera

Lobo Hill in the backround

THE KOPJES (ROCKY OUTCROPS)

The underlying geology of the Short Grass Plains consists mostly of *Precambrian* gneisses with some granites. Evidence of these rocks are the characteristic kopjes (inselbergs or rocky outcrops) protruding above the surface. They have proved resistant to the elements over millions of years. The following kopjes are easily accessible by road:

South Gol Kopjes and Naabi Hill
South-east Barafu Kopjes
South-west Moru Kopjes
Central Maasai Kopjes, Simba Kopjes

A typical kopje in the SNP

THE RIVERS

The large animal population in the Serengeti requires enough water to sustain them all year round. The sources are scattered throughout the park and they hold their water for different times, allowing for a rotational grazing system that is naturally controlled. The rivers in the Serengeti are mostly seasonal but the Mara River in the north contains water all year round. There are a number of rivers, some springs, two permanent lakes and a number of seasonal pans that appear during the rains. The following is a summary of the watersheds of the Serengeti (see map on pg 12 for locations):

Rivers in the north of the park *Mara, Bologonja, Upper Grumeti, Rotari, Bololedi Rivers.* **Grumeti/Mara River systems** These two rivers form important features of the Serengeti Ecosystem as they supply water to the migratory herds on their trek north during the dry season. Both rivers flow more or less from east to west and are important reservoirs for aquatic life and water birds. It is interesting to note that the Serengeti is an important catchment area for the Nile River, as both the above rivers flow into Lake Victoria, the source of the Nile.

Mara River

Rivers in the central parts *Seronera, Ngare Nanyuki, Nyabogati, Orangi Rivers.* **Seronera River** The Seronera River system is situated within the Seronera Valley, in the centre of the Serengeti. The Seronera stretches from the Maasai Kopjes in the south-east and joins the Orangi River just west of Banagi Hill. The Orangi eventually joins the Grumeti, which flows westward into Lake Victoria. The Seronera Valley attracts the highest number of resident ungulates and predators in the park, not only because of its permanent surface water, but also because it is situated on an 'ecotone'. An ecotone is a transitional zone, in this case between the Short Grass Plains in the south-east and the tall grass woodlands in the north and west, the significance of which is that it can sustain more plants and animals.

Seronera River as seen from the air

Rivers in the West *Lower Grumeti and Mbalageti Rivers.* **Lower Grumeti River**

The Lower Grumeti is the single most important river in the western corridor. Although it becomes very dry at times, there are permanent pools of water that can sustain a large resident population. Between May and August it provides an important water source to the migratory animals and one can see thousands of Wildebeests and Zebras crossing the Grumeti, defying the danger of the monstrous Crocodiles that inhabit it.

Mbalageti River The Mbalageti River runs into Lake Victoria and is situated in the west and south-west of the Serengeti. The Mbalageti and its tributaries form a very important resource for the resident fauna and flora. It is also a very important early dry season migratory route and dry season retreat because of permanent water and the abundance of grazing. This area boasts the highest concentration of Topi in the world. It is also known as one of the few remaining refuges for the African Hunting Dog, Roan Antelope and the Patas Monkey. Some cultural sites, associated with the Hadzabe tribe, have been discovered along this river. Access to the area is via the Musabi road that branches off from the main Seronera-Ndabaka road, 53km west of Seronera. It is also possible to access this area from Moru Kopjes, taking the Mamarehe road west and crossing the Duma River. At present the road system in this area is not well developed.

Lower Grumeti River

Rivers in the south-west *Simiyu, Duma, Mbalageti Rivers.* **Simiyu and Duma Rivers**

The headwaters of the Simiyu and Duma Rivers lie entirely within the Serengeti and the Maswa Game Reserve. They flow westward to Lake Victoria and form an important water supply for people and their livestock outside the conservation areas. Within the conservation areas the rivers are protected and provide important refuge to water birds and other aquatic life.

Mbalageti River The lower Mbalageti is an important water source in the south-west of the park (see previous section for more details on the Mbalageti River).

TOPOGRAPHY, GEOLOGY & SOILS

THE LAKES

Lake Ndutu and Lake Magadi in the south Lake Ndutu (also called Lagarja) and Lake Magadi have formed lakes in a shallow basin. The elevation at Lake Ndutu is ±1 600m above sea level. The surrounding areas are slightly higher at 1 640m to the north and 1 700m to the south. The water of the lakes is very shallow and much of it evaporates during the dry season, resulting in dry, grey-white salt pans. The alkaline pans attract birds throughout the year since many water birds, especially Flamingos, show a preference for saline lakes.

Lake Ndutu with Lenakarut Crater in the backround

THE SPRINGS

Turner Springs Turner Springs is located 16km to the east of Seronera head-quarters. The flow from Turner Springs empties into the Ngare Nanyuki River, which eventually flows into the Orangi River north of Banagi Hill. The Orangi River later flows into the Grumeti River, which eventually flows into Lake Victoria.

THE MARSHES

Ndabaka Marsh Driving from Kirawira to Ndabaka Gate, one actually crosses a marsh. However, the road has been built up and one can cross the marsh without any difficulty.

TOPOGRAPHY, GEOLOGY & SOILS

THE GEOLOGICAL TIME CHART

ERA	PERIOD	EPOCH	BEGAN (millions of years ago)	
CENOZOIC	QUARTERNARY	Holoscene	0,01 (10 000 years ago)	Modern Man
		Pleistocene	1,6	Stone-age Man
	TERTIARY	Pliocene	5,3	Mammals, elephants, earliest hominids
		Miocene	23	Flowering plants ancestral dogs, bears
		Oligocene	34	Ancestral pigs, apes
		Eocene	53	Ancestral horses, cattle, elephants
		Palaeocene	65	Horses, cattle, elephants appear
MESOZOIC	CRETACEOUS		135	Extinction of dinosaurs mammals and flowering plants appear
	JURASSIC		205	Dinosaurs and ammonites abundant, birds and mammals appear
	TRIASSIC		250	Flying reptiles and dinosaurs
PALAEOZOIC	PERMIAN		300	Rise of reptiles and amphibians, conifers and beetles appear
	CARBONIFEROUS		355	First reptiles, winged insects
	DEVONIAN		410	First amphibians and ammonites, earliest trees and spiders
	SILURIAN		438	First spore-bearing land plants, earliest known coral reefs
	ORDOVICIAN		510	First fish-like vertebrates
	CAMBRIAN		570	Fossils first appear
PRECAMBRIAN			4 600	Sponges, worms, algae, bacteria, oldest known traces of life

Geological time chart

TOPOGRAPHY, GEOLOGY & SOILS

17

TOPOGRAPHY, GEOLOGY & SOILS

The Precambrian and the Cambrian
The *Precambrian* era is the oldest geological era, representing ±4 000 000 000 (4 billion) years before the the *Palaeozoic* era. The *Palaeozoic* era started about 570 million years ago and lasted for about 320 million years. The *Cambrian* epoch represents the first 60 million years of the *Palaeozoic* era and it ended with the *Permian* epoch. The underlying rocks of the Serengeti were mainly formed during the *Precambrian* era, in other words they are more than 570 million years old. Some of them are much older than that, like the rocks west of Seronera, which are estimated to be 2 500 million years old.

Formation of the underlying rocks of the Serengeti
Although it is very difficult for geologists to determine the exact geological processes that took place so many millions of years ago, the following offers a possible explanation based on Pickering, 1993:

More than 500 million years ago the entire region was covered with water, forming a huge sea into which sand and mud were deposited. The weight caused the ocean floor to sag and with more deposits many thousands of metres of layers accumulated. The first layers were compacted to form mudstones, sandstones and shale. The weight caused the rocks to become folded and some changed chemically. The sandstones folded and re-crystallised to form quartzite. The mudstones and shale were converted to quartz, feldspar, mica, hornblende, kianite and garnet. At the same time molten rock began to push its way up through the existing rock. The latter solidified to form granite. The shales and mudstones changed chemically and mixed with layers of granite to form gneisses.

The Quaternary
The *Quaternary* is the most recent period of geological time and the *Pleistocene* denotes the first epoch of the *Quaternary*. This era is characterised by the evolution of man, which coincides with the formation of the Ngorongoro highlands. The volcanic activity in this area resulted in the build-up of layers of volcanic tuft, some of which was deposited in the direction of the prevailing winds to form endless plains. The most notable of these are the Serengeti Plains which stretch from the Gol Mountains to the Seronera Valley.

Formation of the hills
Most of the hills in the Serengeti consist of *Precambrian* volcanic rocks. The underlying rocks west of Seronera consist of *Precambrian* volcanic rocks and banded ironstone, which form part of the Tanganyika Shield. As mentioned above, these are ±2 500 million years old. These rocks are mainly obscured by subsequently formed sedimentary and meta-sedimentary rocks from the late *Precambrian* era. The upper layer consists of more recent alluvial deposits such as dark, heavy clays, also known as black cotton soil. The lighter soils in the area are mainly derived from sandstones and quartzite.

Formation of the kopjes
The kopjes (inselbergs) seen on the Short Grass Plains form part of the underlying rocks of the area, and consist mainly of *Precambrian* gneisses with some granites. They have proved to be more resistant to the elements. Constant exposure to warm and cold caused the rocks to crack near the surface, shedding their layers as though peeling and ultimately resulting in the characteristic, rounded rocks on the kopjes.

SOILS OF THE SERENGETI

The soils in the south-east of the SNP are shallow and alkaline but they become progressively deeper and less alkaline towards the north-west. The soils of the north-western Serengeti are more sandy. Bell (1986) divided the soils of the Serengeti National Park into five groups:

Black cotton soils are associated with bad drainage. This soil type is common in the Seronera area as well as west and south-west of Seronera. Black cotton soils become extremely sticky during the rainy season.

Alluvial soils are associated with rivers and can be found along existing and extinct drainage lines. They consist of a mixture of sand and clay.

Lateritic soils are formed from *Precambrian* ironstones and meta-volcanic rocks. They are found in the central and western sections of the park and are very clayey.

Sandy soils are formed from granite and basement sediments of Bukoban origin.

Sandy soils are mostly found in the north-western section of the park. The soil particles are larger, allowing for good drainage. In the north-western woodlands the soils are generally sandy, shallow and well-drained in the top layer, changing into deep, silty, poorly-drained soils at the bottom.

Calcareous volcanic soils are shallow as a result of their recent volcanic origin and occur on the Short Grass Plains of the SNP. They are also very alkaline and fertile and are covered by a shallow layer of volcanic dust. The fine, powdered dust so typical of Ndutu, Olduvai and the Salei Plains, is a direct result of volcanic ash emitted from the craters. The calcareous tuff formed solidifications or hard layers called 'hard pan' at various depths, giving the soil the ability to retain water close to the surface. The combination of high fertility and its ability to retain surface water, explains why the Short Grass Plains can support such vast numbers of ungulates during the rainy season.

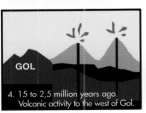
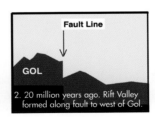
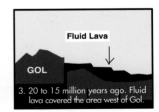

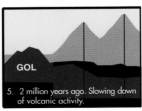
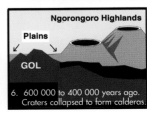

Formation of the Ngorongoro Highlands and the plains during the Quaternary era

Leopard

TOURIST INFORMATION

Lobo Wildlife Lodge

TOURIST INFORMATION

Bookings

If you wish to drive to the Serengeti National Park, it is preferable, but not essential, to book in advance. One can book at Tanzanian National Parks in Arusha by means of the following contacts:

Address: PO Box 3134, Arusha, Tanzania
Tel: (255) (27) 250-3471
Fax: (255) (27) 250-8216
Email: putanapa@habari.co.tz

How to get there

BY AIR

One needs to fly to Kilimanjaro International Airport at Moshe, which is situated at the foot of Mount Kilimanjaro. From there one can take a chartered flight directly to the Serengeti. There is a free shuttle service which will take you to the Impala Hotel in Arusha (it is a central point in town). The distance is 55km. There are also buses and taxis available. Arusha is a tourist town and once there, one can organise to get to the various destinations. However, advance bookings are always advised. The taxi service in town is well developed and easy to find. All the tourist offices are located near the clock-tower in the centre of town.

The airfield at Seronera

BY ROAD

Arusha to the Gregory Rift Escarp
For most people the journey will start at Arusha, a town which is situated in northern Tanzania about midway between Cape Town (in South Africa) and Cairo (in Egypt). The town is situated at the foot of Mount Meru and is surrounded by coffee and banana plantations. It is about 167km east of the Ngorongoro Conservation Area, 260km from the Serengeti entrance gate at Naabi and 320km from Seronera. From the clock-tower, situated in the centre of town, one travels west for ±180km until the road makes a sharp turn left at Makuyuni, marked by a few shops and curio sellers. If you continue south along this road it will take you to Tarangire National Park - the road is tarred all the way there and a visit is highly recommended. If you turn right (west) at Makuyuni, also onto a tarred road, it will take you to the Serengeti. The road has recently been tarred up to the Lodoare Entrance Gate of the Ngorongoro Conservation Area. The rest of the road is gravelled and very corrugated in places.

Some 36km after Makuyuni is the small village of Mto-wa-Mbu, which means 'mosquito creek' in Swahili. Be sure to stock up with fruit and vegetables for your journey ahead. It is also a good place to buy Maasai blankets and curios. Just after the village one crosses a small river at the entrance gate of the Lake Manyara National Park. A visit is highly recommended. There is a variety of accommodation and camping to choose from in and around Mto-wa-Mbu in different price ranges.

The Gregory Rift Escarpment to the Ngorongoro Conservation Area
Almost directly after leaving Mto-wa-Mbu, one ascends a steep escarp (about 600m) which offers a magnificent view of Lake Manyara and the Gregory Rift Valley. It is worth stopping at the summit to enjoy the view and to take photographs. There are also ablution facilities available.

The distance from the escarpment to the next major town, Karatu, is 25km. Here you have a last chance to buy provisions and fill up with fuel. Take note that fuel is available inside the Ngorongoro Conservation Area and the Serengeti. There is also a bank in Karatu where one can change foreign currency. US dollars are accepted at all gates.

The Ngorongoro Conservation Area
Some 15km after Karatu, one reaches the Lodoare Entrance Gate to the Ngorongoro Conservation Area. Daily entrance fees are payable at the gate. Keep in mind that if you are in transit to the Serengeti, you still have to pay the daily fees, but it is well worth it! It is advisable to leave Arusha very early to make the best of your day. There is an information centre at the gate where one can buy guide books and maps.

After leaving Lodoare Gate, one ascends the Ngorongoro Crater wall through magnificent scenery dominated by giant trees. The most common are the tall, straight Pillarwoods (*Cassipourea malosana*), the fluted-stemmed *Nuxia* spp., the dark-stemmed *Diospyros* spp. and the heart-leaved *Croton* Trees, all of which are covered in hanging lichens of the genus *Usnea,* giving one the distinct feeling of driving through a fairy-tale forest. Although non 4x4 vehicles are allowed, this stretch of the road becomes difficult to drive on during the rains. After 6km you will reach the rim where the most incredible view of the Ngorongoro Crater will open up in front of you. One can stop at the Bernhard and Michael Grzimek memorial stone to take photographs - it offers one of the best views of the crater. Further along this road you will see another stone marking their actual graves.

View of Lake Manyara and the Gregory Rift Valley from the escarpment

TOURIST INFORMATION

About 10km after the look-out point, further along the rim of the crater, there is a turn-off to the left to the Ngorongoro tourist office and filling station. If you wish to spend time in the Ngorongoro Conservation Area, you need to announce your arrival there. There is an extra fee to be paid to go into the Ngorongoro Crater.

Keep in mind, self-driving tourists cannot stay over at Naabi Gate, so one has to allow enough time to reach Seronera. From Ngorongoro to Seronera is 140km on a very corrugated road and it takes about 3,5 hours. Take note that you have to reach Seronera before 19h00.

When descending from the highlands, the view is spectacular. One can clearly see the Olduvai Gorge, the Olbalbal Depression and the Gol Mountains on your right and sharply to the left is Sadiman Crater and the much larger Lemakarut Crater. On a clear day one can even see Naabi Hill from the highlands. The distance from the Ngorongoro Crater tourist office to Naabi Gate is 83km.

Naabi Gate At Naabi Gate you announce your arrival and pay entrance fees. If time allows, take the walking trail up the hill to view the surrounding area. It is also a good way to enjoy the kopje fauna and flora at close range. There are ablution facilities and a small shop at the gate as well as picnic tables - the ideal place to enjoy a packed lunch, usually in the company of an array of birds, including

Marabou Storks that solemly wait at the refuse bins for a bite to eat. There bald-headed, hunch-backed appearance and their frequent presence at kills have earned them the name of the 'untertakers' of the African bush.

Naabi Gate to Seronera Seronera is 58km north-west of Naabi and the road is very corrugated in places - make sure all your camping equipment is tied properly. One can see lots of animals along this road, especially in the rainy season, but at times it is totally devoid of game. At ±16km from Naabi Gate you will pass Simba Kopjes which are situated both sides of the road. It is always interesting to drive around the kopjes to scout for Lions and Baboons. Some 26km further you will cross the Seronera River on a low-level bridge.

Seronera area As soon as you arrive at Seronera, look out for the sign to the Seronera Information Centre and Wildlife Tourist Office on your right. Announce your arrival at the office and they will allocate and direct you to a camping site.

Naabi Gate to Lake Ndutu As there are no public camping sites at Lake Ndutu, it will be necessary to link up with an established mobile company to be able to stay at a special camp site. After paying entrance fees at Naabi Gate, drive back on the Ngorongoro road for 4km, then 15km to the west where you will see the Lake. It is 8km further to the Wildlife Tourist Office.

The main road from Naabi Gate to Seronera

CAMPING

There are only two public camp sites in the Serengeti, one at Seronera and one at Lobo. If you join a registered mobile safari company, you have the advantage of staying in a special camp site, separate from the public camp site. These operators are usually very well informed about the migration and local animal movements.

Seronera area You have to announce your arrival at the tourist office near the information centre where you will be allocated and directed to a camping site. The public camping site is about 5km to the east and consists of a number of separate sites. There is one ablution block with showers, toilets and basins to do your laundry and a hosepipe to fill water containers. Some of the public camps are not close to the ablutions so, at night, be sure to use a vehicle because of the danger of wild animals.

Lobo area The camping site at Lobo is situated on the northern side of Lobo Kopje with a magnificent view of the area. There is a pit latrine but no shower facilities - a portable shower is recommended. Predators like to use the flat, open ground for hunting at night, so take care not to walk around after dark.

Lobo public camping site

Joining a mobile safari group in the Serengeti can be a fancy affair. One can camp in complete comfort as each tent has its own ablutions. This outfit belongs to Unique Safaris (see pg 175 for contact details)

TOURIST INFORMATION

25

TOURIST INFORMATION

LODGES

Take note: Advanced bookings are essential for all the lodges below. See pg 175 for contact details.

Lake Ndutu area

There is no lodge on the Serengeti side of Lake Ndutu, only Ndutu Lodge on the Ngorongoro side.

Kusina Camp is situated inside the Serengeti, about 40km south-east of Lake Ndutu. It is a luxury camp in a very secluded area near Silkum Springs.

Seronera area

Seronera Wildlife Lodge is close to the Seronera Information Centre, on the other side of the road. It is built on a kopje and the rocks blend in with the building, giving it a wonderful atmosphere and a beautiful view.

Serena Lodge is 13km to the west of Seronera via the back road and 24km away via the main road. It is very luxurious and is situated on the Kyabatero Hills, offering a spectacular view of the surrounding plains.

Western corridor - Kirawira area

Kirawira Serena Tented Camp is situated on the Simiti Hills, overlooking the Grumeti Valley. The accommodation consists of very luxurious tents. It is only 7km away from the Grumeti River where the Wildebeest and Zebra cross during the migration.

Grumeti Lodge is situated on the northern side of the main road and just north of the Grumeti River, near the airstrip. It is popular during the migration because of being only 2km from the Grumeti River where the migratory animals cross.

Moru Kopjes area

Sopa Lodge is a beautiful lodge with one of the best views in the Serengeti National Park. It is a luxury lodge situated high on the Nyaruboro Hills north-west of the Moru Kopjes. During the late rainy season and early dry season, this area becomes alive with game and it is an excellent place to see Lions. The migration moves through the Moru Kopjes area during March to May, but game viewing is good throughout the year.

Serena Lodge

Lobo area

Lobo Lodge is situated high up on the Lobo Kopjes, offering a magnificent view. It is built from rock, blending in perfectly with the surroundings. It is especially rewarding during the migration, from July to October, but game viewing is good throughout the year.

Lobo Lodge

Migration Camp is situated 21km west of Lobo Kopje on the Grumeti River - an excellent place to enjoy the migration later in the year (July to October). Because of the permanent water there is game throughout the year.

Klein's Camp is situated just north of Klein's Gate on the western boundary. It is a luxury camp and is a hotspot from August to December, when the migratory animals first move up north to the Masai Mara Game Reserve and then back again.

Best season to visit

One can visit the Serengeti National Park any time of year, depending on where the migratory herds of Wildebeest and Zebra can be viewed.

Dry season (May to August) In most other game parks in Africa, it is generally accepted that winter is the best time as the water is scarce and animals are forced to congregate at permanent water sources. In the Serengeti they also go to the permanent water sources but are constantly on the move. One must always try to plan your trip according to where the migratory herds are at that particular time. Keep in mind that the plains become completely devoid of game during the dry season and it is better to visit the western corridor or the northern section of the park during this time. See pg 98 for more details on the annual migration. If you visit in winter, be prepared for a dry, scorched landscape. However, this is also the time to see the dramatic crossing of the rivers by the migratory herds further north in the park.

Rainy season (September to May) In summer one can see the migratory herds on the Short Grass Plains and in the Ndutu area. This is also the time when they have their young and there is a lot of predator activity. If you are a plant lover, summer is definitely the time to visit. Everything turns bright green and the wild flowers and trees seem to explode into colour, contributing greatly to the beautiful scenery, especially when in contrast with the heavy rain clouds in the backround.

The Seronera River is an important water source for migratory animals during the early dry season

27

Vulture

PLACES TO SEE

A hazy landscape at Rongai with Green Thorn Trees (Balanites aegyptiaca) in the foreground

Lobo area The Lobo area consists of a mosaic of vegetation types that can support a variety of game. The area has permanent water in the Ngare Naironya Springs and in pools in the Upper Grumeti River, providing sufficient water for the migratory and resident animals. From July to November the bulk of the migratory herds moves through the area, first north to the Masai Mara Game Reserve and then south again to return to the Short Grass Plains. Lobo area is known for its high concentrations of Lions and prides of over 30 are common.

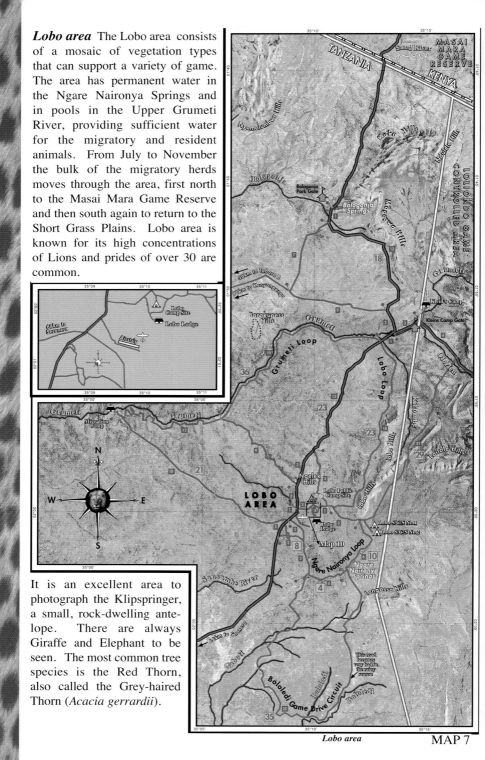

It is an excellent area to photograph the Klipspringer, a small, rock-dwelling antelope. There are always Giraffe and Elephant to be seen. The most common tree species is the Red Thorn, also called the Grey-haired Thorn (*Acacia gerrardii*).

Lobo area   MAP 7

Recommended routes If time allows, it is worth doing all the loops. The loop passing the Ngare Naironya Springs is highly recommended. The Bololedi loop, which is much longer and further south, is also interesting but is not always accessible during the rainy season. This loop will take at least three hours to complete. The Grumeti River loop is also very interesting, but take note that the road is bad in places and may takes up to five hours to complete. The Lobo Hills road, which crosses the plains west of the hills up to Klein's Gate, is very scenic and one is likely to see Elephant there.

Best season The dry season is especially rewarding as the migratory herds pass through from July to November. However, any time of year is suitable as there is a large resident animal population.

THE KLIPSPRINGER ANTELOPE

The Klipspringer's hooves are tiny and stiletto-like - literally the size of your two little fingers held together. The hooves are rubbery underneath to ensure that they do not slip whilst jumping from rock to rock. Another interesting thing about the Klipspringer is that, unlike other antelope, its eyes are forward-looking, situated more to the front of its head instead of on the side. This allows them to have binocular vision, much like humans and other primates, enabling them to judge distance.

Lobo is one of the few places in the Serengeti where the Klipspringer is common

This is a typical scene around Lobo. Lions are abundant in this area

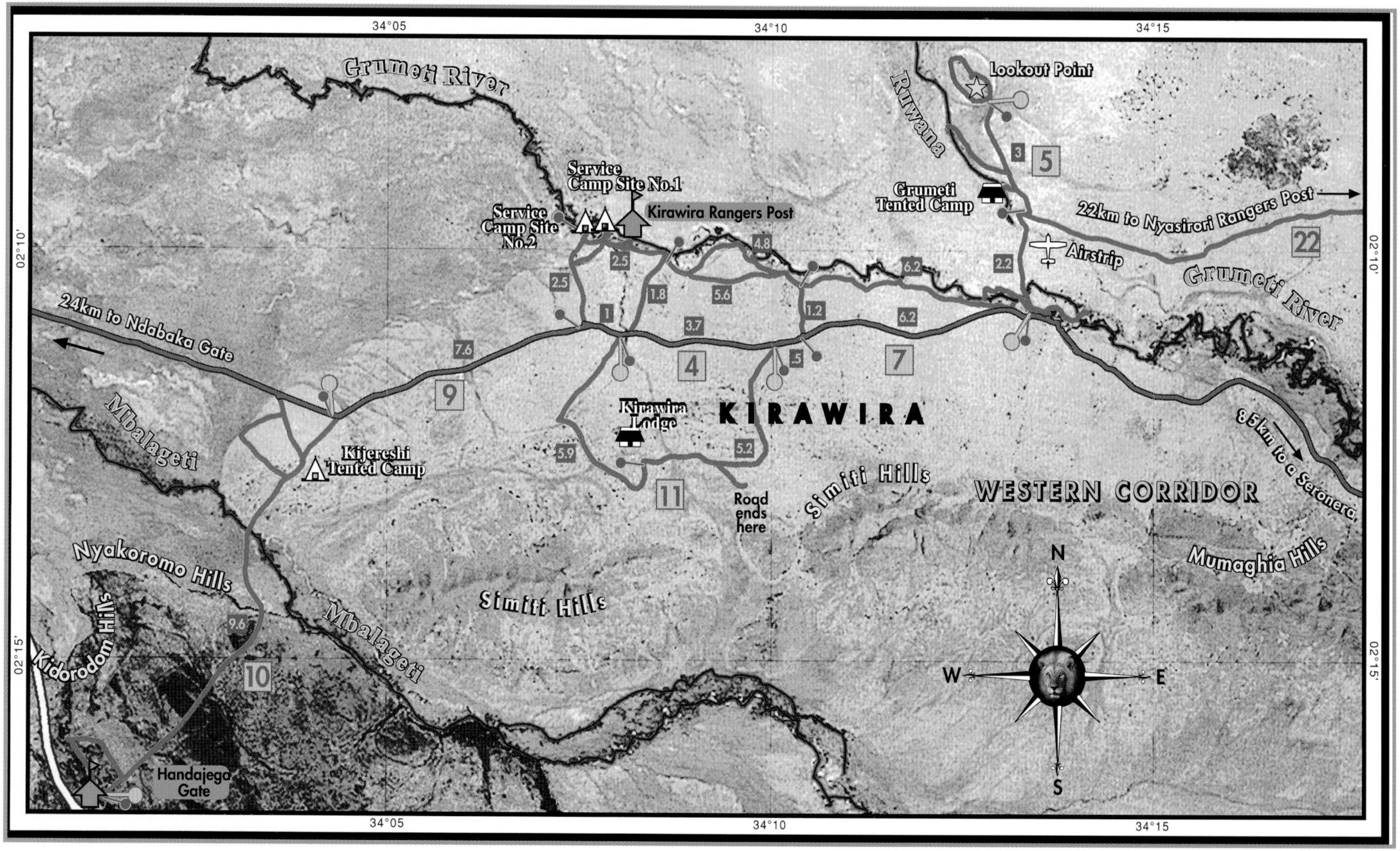

The Kirawira game drive circuit in the western corridor

MAP 8

This area is very popular during winter (between May and August) when the Wildebeest migration crosses the Grumeti River. The phenomenon of thousands of Wildebeests and Zebras fearlessly plunging into the crocodile-ridden waters of the Grumeti has been documented over and over, but actually witnessing it, makes your heart pound and your emotions soar. You feel honoured and humbled at the same time by this death-defying force of nature, in which the survival of the species takes precedence and each individual is willing to forfeit life to accomplish that goal.

Permanent pools of water in the Grumeti ensure a large resident population of animals in the western corridor. Cheetahs, Lions, Hyenas and Leopards are plentiful. The Handajega and Mbalageti River areas have the highest population of Topi left in Africa. It is also a refuge for African Hunting Dogs, Roan Antelope and the rare Patas Monkey. The Crocodiles of the Grumeti are gigantic - that alone is worth seeing.

Recommended routes Most of the action takes place along the loops near the Grumeti River in the Kirawira area. As the game-drive circuit is relatively small, all the routes in the area are recommend. The road north of the Grumeti leading to Kirawira II Rangers Post, passes through open plains and there are often predators at Nyasirori Dam. One can cross to the main road by going south from the Rangers Post, but check with the game rangers if the bridge is in good condition, as it is often damaged by floods.

Best season The best time to visit is during the peak of the migration, from May to July, but because of permanent water pools, any season is rewarding.

Grumeti River

The Crocodiles of the Grumeti are exceptionally large

PLACES TO SEE – WESTERN CORRIDOR

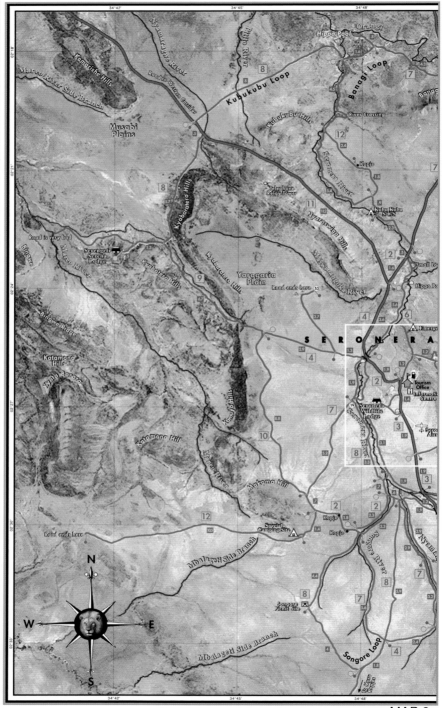

The Senorera game drive circuit

MAP 9a

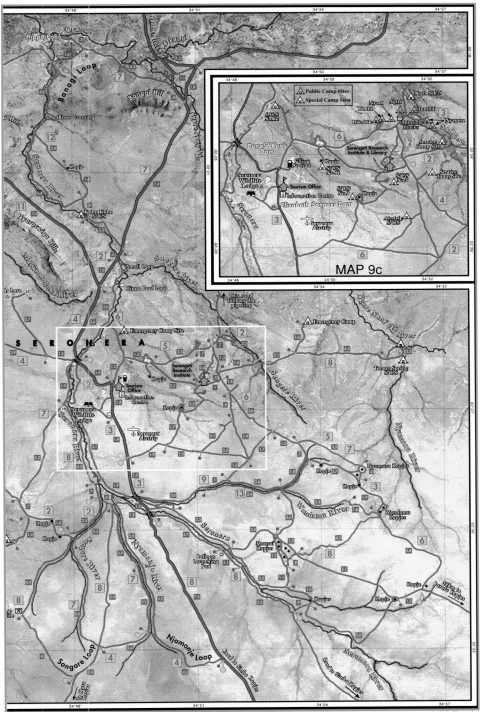

MAP 9c

MAP 9b

Seronera is the most important tourist destination in the Serengeti because of its easy access and good infra-structure. From an ecological point of view, the Seronera area is also important as it forms a transitional zone between open grassland in the south-east and wooded grassland in the north-west. Such a transitional zone is called an 'ecotone', the significance of which is that it supports a higher diversity of fauna and flora and a larger animal populaion. The permanent surface water flowing through the Seronera River and its tributaries supports the resident as well as migratory animals. The Turner Springs, 11km east of Seronera, is also an important source of fresh water. Although Leopards are very secretive and nocturnal, Seronera is one of the best places to see them. It is also one of the best places to see Elephant in the Serengeti.

The two most common trees at Seronera are the flat-topped Umbrella Thorn (*Acacia tortilis*) that dots the open plains and the yellow-barked Fever Tree (*Acacia xanthophloea*) that grows along the rivers. On the edges of the plains one can see the characteristic Sausage Trees (*Kigelia africana*) which almost all have a straight Giraffe browse-line. The flowers are large, red and cup-shaped and the fruits are sausage-shaped, almost one metre long.

Leopard

Seronera is one of the best places to see Elephants in the SNP

Seronera Valley

PLACES TO SEE - SERONERA

A Lioness taking refuge from the flies in a Sausage Tree

During the rainy season the Lions are plagued by flies and they often seek refuge in the Sausage Trees because of the lack of thorns and the thick, horizontal branches.

The vegetation on the rocky outcrops is varied and different to the surrounding vegetation. The most common kopje plants are the succulent Candelabra (*Euphorbia candelabrum*), the trailing Wild Grape (*Cissus quadrangularis*), the Sandpaper Bush (*Cordia ovalis*) and the Strangler Fig (*Ficus thonningii*). See pg 61 for more details on the vegetation.

Recommended routes All the routes along the rivers in the Seronera Valley are recommended and no matter how many times you do them, they always have something new to offer. Other worthwhile drives are to Turner Springs, even though one cannot see the springs as such. There are often Lion to be seen at Maasai Kopjes. One can also go the Songore picnic site where you can get out and stretch your legs or enjoy a packed lunch. The Banagi Hill loop which goes to the Hippo Pool is also highly recommended. You have a very good chance of seeing Kirk's Dik-dik along the Banagi loop.

Other, slightly further areas that one can visit from Seronera on a day trip are Moru Kopjes, Lake Magadi, Maasai Kopjes, Simba Kopjes and the western corridor. These are all described in detail further on.

Best season Any time of the year is good in the Seronera area because of the permanent water. A portion of the migratory herds move through the area from about March to June.

The picnic site on the Songore loop

SERONERA INFORMATION CENTRE

Seronera Information Centre Your visit to the Serengeti is not complete without a visit to the Seronera Information Centre. It is situated next to the wildlife offices (see map on pg 34). There is a very informative open-air exhibit situated on the kopje. Each exhibit is accompanied by a written explanation, much like an outdoor museum.

Picnic tables at the Seronera Information Centre

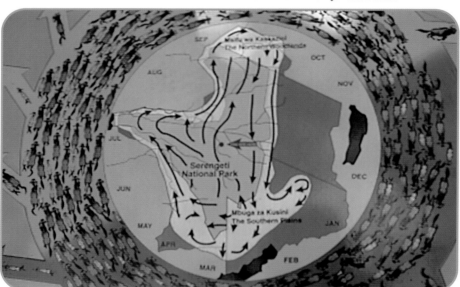

A depiction of the Wildebeest migration at the Seronera Information Centre

A 'wave' of Wildebeest moving en masse on the plains

PLACES TO SEE – SERONERA

The Hyraxes on the kopje have become very used to humans, providing an opportunity to observe and photograph them closely. Take note that there are two different kinds of Hyraxes - the brown ones are Rock Hyraxes and the slightly larger, grey ones are Tree Hyraxes. The Tree Hyraxes can often be seen in the trees instead of on the rocks. The colourful lizard, so common on the rocks, is the Agama Lizard which feeds on insects. Only the male has the bright, pink and purple colours, the female being smaller and quite drab in comparison.

Tree Hyrax

Rock Hyrax

Agama Lizard

It is possible to order tea, coffee or soft drinks and enjoy a packed lunch at the centre as there are tables and shade available for this purpose. As soon as you sit down a menagerie of birds descends in the hope of getting a free lunch. They offer the ideal opportunity for close-up photography and for identification at your leisure. The following are some of the birds frequently seen at the Information Centre.

Superb Starling

D'Arnaud's Barbet

Grey-capped Social Weaver

Speckled-fronted Weaver

Rufous Sparrow

Green-winged Pytilla

Red-billed Fire-finch

Purple Grenadier

Laughing Dove

PLACES TO SEE - SERONERA

There are also other animals that provide free entertainment. The Black-faced Monkeys are not always the most welcome of visitors as they are usually up to mischief, their main objective being to rob you of your lunch. Nevertheless, it is interesting to watch as they plan their strategy with their intelligent eyes flicking around, but beware, they act fast and accurately and when you least expect it. The Banded and Dwarf Mongooses are also fascinating to watch. They always seem to be in a hurry as they dart around in their endless search for food, scratching here, then there, whilst happily chattering away until an alarm squeal makes them disappear in an instant. One can easily spend a few hours at the centre without a boring moment.

Banded Mongoose

Dwarf Mongoose

Black-faced Vervet Monkey

Balloon safaris One of the best experiences one can hope to have in the Serengeti is a balloon ride. There is nothing to compare with the sensation of feeling as free as a bird and enjoying the scenery in utter silence whilst soaring weightlessly through the air. At intervals the burners roar, producing the flames and hot air that keep the balloon aloft, followed by complete and utter silence.

One can book a balloon safari at any of the hotels and they will take you to the meeting place at the Serengeti Wildlife Lodge. The group meets long before day-break and a feeling of anticipation hangs in the air as everyone is introduced, enjoying a warm beverage before leaving for the place of departure. It is fascinating to watch how the team unfold the balloon and get it ready for launching. The ride itself is about one and a half hours long. Afterwards you are treated to a champagne breakfast on the Serengeti Plains in the company of your pilot and fellow passengers. It is simply magic!

A typical Seronera scene

Balloon safari

PLACES TO SEE – SERONERA

Common Diadem - female
(Hypolimnas misippus)

Common Diadem - male
(Hypolimnas misippus)

Blue Pansy
(Junonia oenone)

Guinea Fowl
(Hamanumida daedalus)

Grass Yellow
(Eurema sp.)

Dotted Border
(Mylothris agathine)

Painted Lady
(Vanessa cardui)

Brown-veined White
(Belenois aurota aurota)

Queen Purple Tip
(Colotis regina)

Foxy Charaxes - upper side
(Charaxes candiope)

Foxy Charaxes - underside
(Charaxes candiope)

Bushveld Charaxes
(Charaxes achaemenes)

African Monarch
(Danaus chrysippus)

Citrus Swallowtail
(Papilio demodocus)

Scarlet Tip
(Colotis danae)

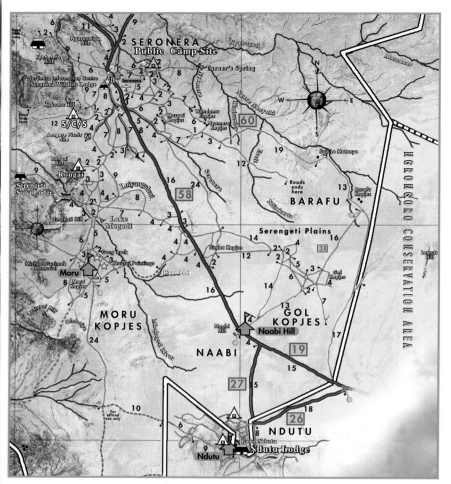

The Short Grass Plains

MAP 10

Wildebeest walking across the Short Grass Plains

Short Grass Plains

The Short Grass Plains are what the Serengeti is famous for. This is certainly one of the most interesting areas to be enjoyed. The soil type is of volcanic origin, the result of layer upon layer of volcanic ash emitted from the volcanoes that formed the Ngorongoro highlands. In places the underlying rocks protrude above the surface and have eroded to form the kopjes so typical of the landscape. The soils are fertile, supporting vast numbers of game - up to 2 million animals during the rains. During the dry season (May to October), the plains appear to be a vast stretch of nothingness, almost totally devoid of animals. In early summer the migratory animals return to have their young and the plains become alive again, offering dramatic wildlife experiences that visitors will never forget. The Plains stretch from the Gol Mountains to the Seronera Valley and from the north-east of Barafu Kopjes to Moru Kopjes to south of Lake Ndutu.

Recommended routes The Short Grass Plains of the Serengeti lie to the south-east of Seronera, stretching from Barafu Kopjes to Maasai Kopjes to Moru Kopjes to Lake Ndutu, all of which are described in more detail in the following pages.

Best season The best time of year to visit the Short Grass Plains is during the peak of the birth season - January to February - but the migratory herds often remain in the area until late March to the end of April.

Zebras on the Short Grass Plains

The routes are described in more detail in the following sections:

There are camping sites at Naabi Gate but they are not generally open to self-drivers, only to licenced, mobile operators. When the migratory herds move through the area, Naabi Hill offers an excellent vantage point from which to view them, especially if you follow the trail up the hill. Naabi Hill is also a good place to see Cheetah. If time allows, take the walking trail up the hill to view the surrounding area. It is also a good way to enjoy the vegetation up close because one cannot walk around on the kopjes elsewhere in the park, except at Seronera Information Centre. The colourful male Agama Lizards (*Agama agama*) and the smaller, grey-brown females sun themselves on the rocks and offer excellent photo opportunities. In summer the kopje becomes alive with butterflies (see pg 41 for identification photographs of butterflies). There are ablution facilities and a small shop at the gate as well as picnic tables - the ideal place to enjoy a packed lunch.

Recommended routes Naabi is only 27km from Ndutu, 19km from Gol Kopjes, 33km from Barafu Kopjes and 16km from Simba Kopjes. During the rainy season, Naabi is an excellent choice as you will have quick access to all the surrounding areas.

Best season The best season is during the rainy months when the migratory herds move through the area. During the dry season the plains may be very quiet, but there is alway something to see at Naabi Hill.

Picnic tables at Naabi Gate

Superb Starling

Igama Lizard

The beginning of the Kopje trail at Naabi Gate

Maasai Kopjes

The Maasai Kopjes are near Seronera, only 12km to the south-east. It is the perfect place for an early morning or late afternoon drive. Predators, especially Lions are abundant in the area. One can often see Buffalo here as it is reasonably close to permanent water.

Recommended routes Maasai Kopjes are close to each other, enabling one to explore all the roads around the kopjes.

Best season Like everywhere on the Serengeti plains, the rainy season is usually more exciting.

Maasai Kopjes

Simba Kopjes

Simba Kopjes are situated right next to the main road, 32km from Seronera and 16km from Naabi Gate. There is always something to see.

Recommended routes Drive around all the kopjes as your chance of seeing Lions is very good. Take note that the kopjes are situated both sides of the road and it is worth exploring all of them. Also do the road to the west that follows a side-branch of the Mbalageti River, all the way up to the Hippo Pool which is 7km from Simba Kopjes. The end of the road is indicated by white stones and you are not allowed to continue beyond this point. It is well worth the effort to drive to the Hippo Pool and back.

Best season The best season is during the rainy season but since it is situated along the main road one does not have to make a special effort to get there. Therefore, any season is good.

Lions at Simba Kopjes

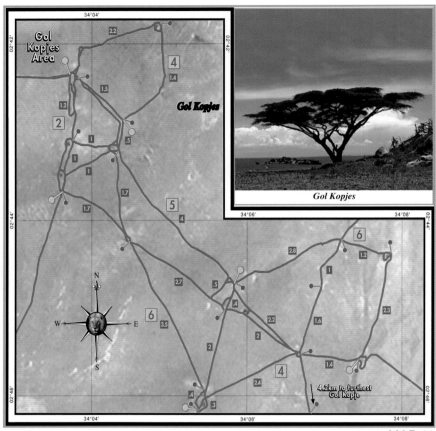

The Gol Kopjes game drive circuit

MAP 11

The Gol Kopjes are situated north-east of Naabi Gate. When the migration moves through the area, this is one of the best places to see predators and it contains critical denning sites. The roads lead to all the kopjes and you are bound to find several prides of Lion. The Lions usually lounge around on the kopjes where they have a perfect vantage point from which to contemplate their next meal. Cheetahs and Hyenas are very common in the area. Birds, especially raptors, are prolific in the area.

Augur Buzzard

It is a good place to see the Greater and Lesser Kestrels, the Augur Buzzard and the Tawny Eagle.

Recommended routes Each kopje is different and worth exploring and as the distances are short, all roads are recommended.

Best season The best season is during the rainy season when the migratory animals move through the area. During the dry season, the area surrounding the kopjes becomes completely empty of game.

Barafu Kopjes

Although the kopjes themselves are not particularly attractive, both routes, the one from Seronera to Barafu and the one from Gol Kopjes to Barafu are absolutely spectacular. One needs a guide to go to Barafu and this can be organised at the wildlife office at Seronera. From Seronera one drives in a south-easterly direction through vast plains until one reaches the Ngare Nanyuki River, 41km from Seronera. Here the scenery changes to Riverine Acacia veld consisting mainly of Fever Trees (*Acacia xanthophloea*). Shortly before reaching the river, one passes a prominent kopje called Soit le Motonye, meaning 'rock in the water' - an indication that the area becomes flooded. The Barafu Gorge is an important water catchment area and an important predator breeding site, especially for Cheetah. Although it is called a 'gorge', it is no more than a slight indent in the flat landscape or a dry river bed.

From Barafu to Gol Kopjes one crosses the true Short Grass Plains of the Serengeti which stretch endlessly, resembling a well-kept lawn. The game in this area is plentiful and apart from all the other plains game, one can see huge herds of Eland. The Eland are not used to vehicles and they do not allow one to approach closely. There are seasonal pans at intervals on the plains where large herds of ungulates concentrate. Do not attempt to go to Barafu without a guide as it is strictly against the rules and there are wildlife officers on constant patrol at Barafu who will follow your approach from miles away.

Recommended routes One can only do the two routes described above. I suggest you drive from Seronera to Barafu and from there to Gol Kopjes as both routes are very exciting. There is no game drive circuit at Barafu.

Best season The best season is during the rainy season when the migration passes through the area. During the dry season the plains may be completely empty.

The Barafu Gorge

The road between Gol and Barafu Kopjes

Herds of Eland can be seen on the Short Grass Plains during the rainy season, but they are very nervous and do not allow a close approach

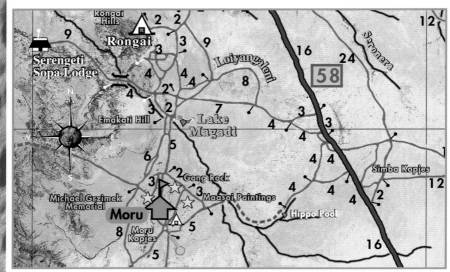

The Lake Magadi game drive circuit

MAP 12

Lake Magadi

Flamingos often come to feed at Lake Magadi

Lake Magadi is near Moru Kopjes. It is a very scenic area and an excellent place to see water birds. In summer there are usually Flamingos, although they do not nest there. The birdlife at Lake Magadi is similar to that of Lake Ndutu (see pg 60 for identification photos of the most common species).

Recommended routes There are three major routes of interest in this area. The loop around Emakati Hill is very rewarding as one can see Elephant and Giraffe and a variety of other game, the Baboons being the most entertaining. The drive to Sopa Lodge is also interesting as you cross two rivers, the Loiyangaleni River and the Mbalageti, where there is usually animal activity. One of my favourite loops is the Loiyangaleni River loop where one often sees Lions. It is also one of the few places where one can see the rare Bohor Reedbuck. In the Rongai area, along the road leading back to Seronera, one passes through an area of tall grassland dotted with trees. The most common large tree in this area is the Green Thorn (*Balanites aegyptiaca*) which has thorny branches and a distinct, oval, flattened canopy (see pg 65 for more details).

The Whistling Thorn (*Acacia depranolobium*) is also common in the area. This tree has galls at the thorn bases which are inhabited by ants. The openings in the galls produce a whistling sound when the wind blows (see photo below and pg 65 for more details).

Best season The best season is during the late rainy season to the early dry season when the migratory herds move through the area. However, a visit any time of year is recommended, as there are always resident Giraffe, Baboons and other game. The birdlife is also excellent.

Whistling Thorn (note the galls at the thorn bases)

Green Thorn (Balanites aegyptiaca)

Whistling Thorn (Acacia depranolobium)

PLACES TO SEE - LAKE MAGADI

49

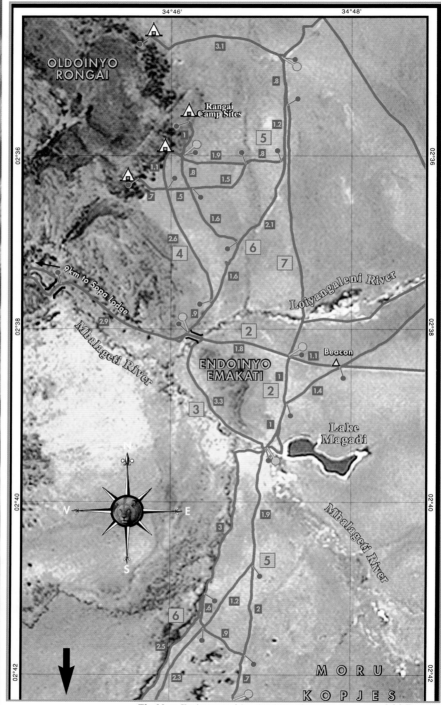

34°46'   34°48'

02°36

OLDOINYO
RONGAI

3.1

.8

1.2

Rangai
Camp Sites

5

1.9   .8

1.1

.8   1.5

.7   .5

1.6

2.1

2.6

4   6   7

9km to Sopa lodge

1.6

2.9

.9

2

Loiyangaleni River

1.8

1.1   Beacon

ENDOINYO
EMAKATI

Mbalageti River

1

2   1.4

3.3

3

1

Lake
Magadi

N

1.9

N   E   3

5   Mbalageti River

S

1.2

6   .6   2

.9

2.5

6   M O R U

2.3   7

K O P J E S

02°36

02°38

02°40

02°42

The Moru Kopjes game drive circuit (north)   MAP 13a

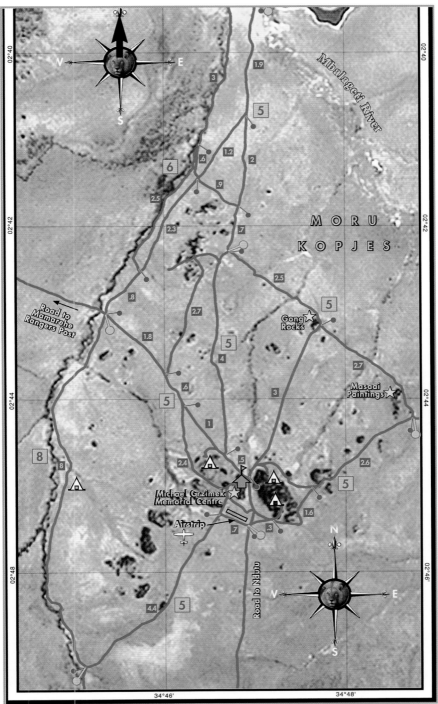

The Moru Kopjes game drive circuit (south)

MAP 13b

The Moru Kopjes area is located on one of the major migratory routes. There is enough surface water, springs, wetlands, forage and mineral licks to support large numbers of animals. As recently as the early 1950s, Maasai pastoralists still lived in the area. On one of the kopjes there are some Maasai rock paintings which serve as evidence of their earlier presence. The patterns on the shields of the Maasai were clan-specific and the paintings were probably a means of communication between clans - a way of leaving their signature and letting other clans know that they were there.

Near the rock paintings one can see the Gong Rocks which consist of large rocks with holes on the vertical side. It has been suggested that the rocks were used as a means of communication to produce a sound to call tribe or clan members together, maybe after a hunt.

The Gong Rocks

Maasai rock paintings at Moru Kopjes area

Close-up of the Gong Rocks. It is said the holes were used to produce a sound to call the clan together

One is not allowed to approach Moru Kopjes from Simba Kopjes in the east. The road has been closed by means of white rocks at the Hippo Pool, which is about 7km west of Simba Kopjes. One has to approach Moru Kopjes from Lake Magadi. The reason for the closure of the road is to enable wildlife officers to guard the area more carefully. There are some Black Rhino in the area which are very closely guarded by wildlife officials against poachers. The rangers have look-out posts on the highest kopjes. So, if you try to sneak in from the east, they will follow your approach from far away. The Rhino project is sponsored by the Frankfurt Zoological Society. (See pg 55 for more details on the Frankfurt Zoological Society and pg 54 for details on the Rhino project.)

Recommended routes The distances between the kopjes are short, therefore all routes can be done in one day. I do recommend a visit to the Michael Grzimek Memorial Museum at the Game Rangers Post as it explains more about the Rhino project. I also suggest a visit to the Maasai Paintings and the Gong Rocks. In both cases it is a very short climb. The drive along the Mbalageti side-branch to the west of Moru Kopjes is also worth doing as there is always activity along the river. The road to the east to Mamarehe Rangers Post is quite negotiable for the first ±10km up to the Nyaruboro Hills.

Best season The best time of year is in summer to early winter, from March to June, when the migration is most likely to pass through.

Moru Kopjes - note the Candelabra Trees
(Euphorbia candelabrum) on the kopjes

This photo was taken at Moru Kopjes during a controlled burning programme

PLACES TO SEE - MORU KOPJES

THE BLACK RHINO PROTECTION PROGRAMME

There are five species of Rhino in the world of which two species are found in Africa - the White Rhino and the Black Rhino. The two last remaining free-ranging Black Rhino populations in Tanzania are at the Ngorongoro Crater and at Moru Kopjes in the Serengeti.

In 1966 there were 108 Rhinos in the Ngorongoro Crater and 69 at Olduvai Gorge.

Between 1974 and 1978 about 700 Black Rhinos were counted in the Serengeti National Park. Along the Seronera River there was one Rhino per 10km^2.

After 1975 Rhino poaching increased with demand for Rhino horn, used as aphrodisiacs in the Far East and to produce dagger handles in north Yemen. With the increase in demand, prices increased and so did the ruthlessness of poachers.

In 1980 there were an estimated 50 to 100 Rhinos left in the Serengeti with ±20 at Moru Kopjes and only 25 to 30 in the Ngorongoro Crater. Not a single Rhino survived in the Olduvai Gorge.

In 1993 there was a further decline and only 14 to 18 Rhinos were counted in the Ngorongoro Crater. Only about five Rhinos were counted in the Serengeti. The once common Black Rhino was now almost extinct in northern Tanzania.

It was time for drastic steps. In November 1993 the Ngorongoro Conservation Area Authority (NCAA) and the Frankfurt Zoological Society (FZS) jointly devised a project proposal for the conservation of Rhinos of the Ngorongoro Crater. In 1995 a similar joint project was initiated between the Tanzanian National Parks (TANAPA) and Frankfurt Zoological Society. Tracking devices were implanted in the horns of the Rhinos to enable wildlife staff to monitor their movement 24 hours per day.

These joint projects have proved very successful thanks to the commitment of the Ngorongoro Conservation Area Authority, the Tanzanian National Parks and the Frankfurt Zoological Society as well as the dedication of the rangers and researchers involved in the project.

This photograph illustrates how tracking devices are implanted in the Rhino's horn

Black Rhino bull

THE FRANKFURT ZOOLOGICAL SOCIETY

Over the last fifty years and more, the Frankfurt Zoological Society has made tremendous contributions to the infrastructure, management and research in the Serengeti National Park. It was founded in 1858 and started off as a Zoological Garden in Frankfurt, Germany. Professor Bernhard Grzimek became the zoo director and president of the society after World War II.

During the early 1950s, Professor Grzimek and his son Michael came to the Serengeti in a small aircraft to do game counts and, in general, to promote the preservation of the Serengeti National Park. They provided the first estimates of the migratory animal numbers and produced the famous book and film 'Serengeti Shall Not Die', making people all over the world aware of the urgent need for conservation. The book was translated in all the major languages. Their real accomplishment was the realisation of their far-sighted goal to preserve functioning ecosystems, a goal that they have achieved with great success.

Sadly, Michael died in 1959 during a survey in the Ngorongoro Crater but his father continued to lobby government to make conservation a priority. He became friends with the then President, Dr Julius Nyerere, and supplied financial support for Government-backed environmental projects. Today, Tanzania is one of the most conservation-orientated countries on earth.

When Professor Grzimek died in 1987, Dr Richard Faust took over as President and today, more than 80 projects in 20 countries, on four continents are supported by the Frankfurt Zoological Society. For more than fifty years the Tanzanian National Parks and the Frankfurt Zoological Society have had an uninterrupted record of close co-operation. One of their greatest accomplishments is the success story of the Black Rhino Protection Programme (read more about this on pg 54). This, and many other projects, were partly made possible by proceeds from 'Serengeti Shall Not Die'. The Society's annual budget for Tanzania, is in excess of 2,5 million German Marks. It has been spread over a variety of projects throughout the country.

Their grave is located on the Ngorongoro Crater rim

Professor Bernhard and Michael Grzimek

PLACES TO SEE - MORU KOPJES

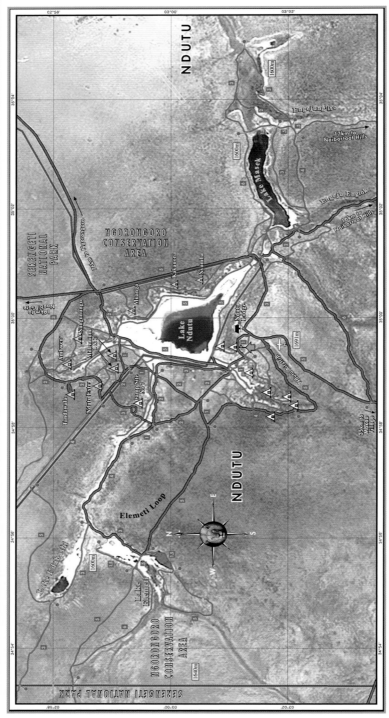

MAP 14

The Lake Ndutu game drive circuit on the Ngorongoro Conservation Area side as well the Serengeti side

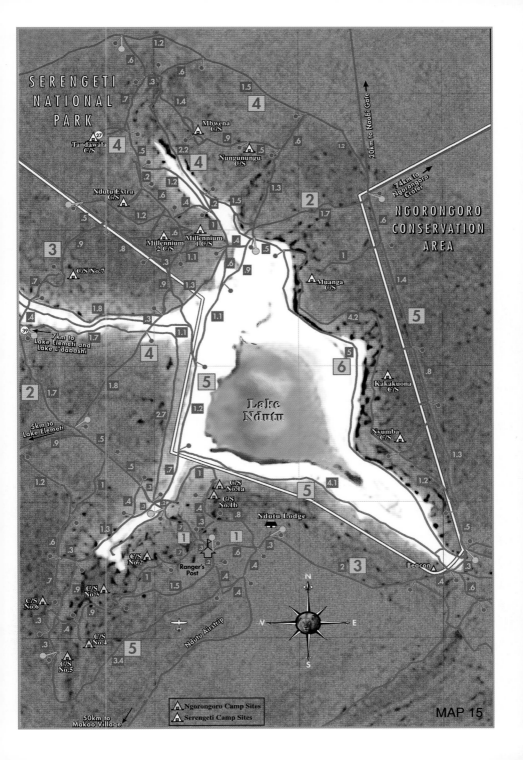

MAP 15

A pregnant female Cheetah drinking at Lake Ndutu

Lake Ndutu is one of the prime destinations in the Serengeti, especially during the rains when the migratory animals concentrate on the Short Grass Plains in the south. During this time, depending on local rains, there are short movements between Gol Kopjes, Naabi, the Ngorongoro Conservation Area, Lake Ndutu and Maswa Game Reserve. There are always at least some Wildebeests and Zebras at Lake Ndutu and the bird-life is spectacular at all times. Lions, Hyenas, Cheetahs and Giraffes are commonly seen.

White Storks are very common at Lake Ndutu

The Wildebeest migratory herds frequent the Ndutu area during the rainy season

The tail end of a stampede accross Lake Ndutu

One of the most exhilarating and heart-rending experiences at Lake Ndutu is a Wildebeest stampede across the lake. This is a phenomenon that occurs at regular intervals and can be triggered by anything, usually by predators. The reason they run across the lake is because it is shallow and it is the shortest way to the other side. In the madness of the moment, calves get seperated from their mothers and as soon as the mothers realise, they turn back, creating a two-way chaos within a cacophony of calls. Without exception, a few calves loose their mothers forever. Lost calves will follow any moving object, especially moving vehicles and they will even walk up to predators. It leaves one feeling totally powerless when they are aggressively rejected by other females whilst uttering their forlorne cries. The calves often lose complete hope and wait motionless in the water until they fall over and die. This is nature's way of eliminating the weakest and preparing the survivors for the even harsher realities of their journey up north.

Recommended routes The distances of the game drive routes are short, so all routes are recommended. The route following the lake's edge is particularly rewarding. Look carefully at the map on pg 57 and make sure that you do not venture into the NCA - the roads can be confusing and rangers on both sides patrol and may ask for your permit. The road between Naabi Gate and Ndutu is also very rewarding during the migration.

Best season Ndutu is good at all times of the year but especially in summer. The migration almost always passes through there in January to March. From March to April one can see large herds of Zebras in the area and the bird life is always good.

Baby Wildebeest often lose their mothers amidst a stampede

59

BIRDS OF LAKE NDUTU

The following are some of the most common water birds at Lake Ndutu:

Greater Flamingo

Lesser Flamingo

White Stork

Three-banded Plover

Blacksmith Lapwing

Black-winged Stilt

Kittlitz's Plover

Common Sandpiper

Ruff

Chestnut-banded Plover

Cape Teal

Spoonbill

Whiskered Tern

Cattle Egret

Hamerkop

PLACES TO SEE – LAKE NDUTU

VEGETATION

Jute Fibre Hibiscus (Hibiscus cannabinus)

Introduction

This section on vegetation is an introduction to the more common plants of the Serengeti, including a few of their interesting uses. The trees, wild flowers and grasses are discussed separately in sub-sections. Identification photographs of the trees and the grasses are provided in alphabetical order according to their scientific names for easier reference. In the case of the wild flowers, the photographs are presented in colour groups - white, green, yellow, pink and blue - and the colour groups are arranged alphabetically.

MAJOR VEGETATION ZONES OF THE SERENGETI NATIONAL PARK

The vegetation of the SNP can be broadly classified into three major vegetation types:

- The Short Grass Plains in the south-east.
- The Broad-leafed Woodland of the north.
- The mosaic of Grassland and Thorn Tree Woodland in the west and south.

There is an ecotone or division that runs roughly through the Seronera Valley, separating the Short Grass Plains from the Thorn Tree and Broad-leafed Woodland. Ecotones have a higher species diversity and can sustain larger numbers of hervbivores, a fact that is well illustrated in the Seronera area.

Most of the Thorntree Woodlands in the Serengeti are dominated by thorny *Acacia* and *Commiphora* species with two exceptions. The woodland in the north-west consists of broad-leafed species dominated by *Terminalia* and *Combretum*. In the Rongai area, south-west of Seronera, the vegetation type is called 'Wooded Grassland' and the dominant woody species in this type of grassland is the Green Thorn (*Balanites aegyptiaca*).

Fireball Lillies (Scadoxus multiflorus)

VEGETATION

Some of the most common tree species in the Serengeti National Park:

Most common trees along the rivers

Acacia brevispica (Prickly Acacia)
Carissa edulis (Num-num)
Cordia ovalis (Sandpaper Bush)
Croton dichogamus (Croton)
Diospyros abyssinica (Giant Diospyros)
Drypetes gerrardii (Hairy drypetes)
Ekebergia capensis (Cape Ash)
Elaeodendron buchananii (Elaeodendron)
Euclea divinorum (Gwarrie bush)
Ficus sycomorus (Sycamore Fig)
Ficus thonningii (Strangler Fig)
Garcinia livingstonei (African Mangosteen)
Grewia bicolor (Two-coloured Grewia / Raisin Bush)
Grewia tennax (Giant Grewia / Raisin Bush)
Olea europaea subsp. africana (Wild Olive)
Schrebera alata (Winged-leaved Wooden Pear)
Strychnos henningsii (Coffee-bean Strychnos)
Tamarindus indica (Tamarind)
Teclea trichocarpa (Furry-fruited Teclea)
Turraea robusta (Honeysuckle tree)
Ziziphus pubescens (Small Jujube)

The most common trees in Broad-leafed Woodland

Acacia hockii
Acacia nilotica (Sweet Thorn)
Boscia angustifolia (Rough-leafed Shepherd's Tree)
Carissa edulis (Num-num)
Combretum molle (Velvet Bushwillow)
Commiphora africana (Poison-grub commiphora)
Cordia ovalis (Sandpaper Bush)
Dombeya rotundifolia (Wild Pear)
Euclea divinorum (Gwarrie Bush)
Euphorbia candelabrum (Candelabra)
Grewia trichocarpa (Wild raison)
Heeria reticulata (Heeria)
Kigelia africana (Sausage Tree)
Lannea stuhlmannii (False Marula)
Lonchocarpus eriocalyx (Broad-leafed Lance-pod)
Olea europaea subsp. africana (Wild Olive)
Pappea capensis (Indaba Tree)
Parinari curatellifolia (Mobola Plum or Grey-apple Tree)
Rhus natanlensis (Natal Rhus)
Schrebera alata (Winged-leafed Wooden Pear)
Sclerocarya birrea (Marula Tree)
Terminalia mollis (Large-leafed Terminalia)

The Acacia trees of the SNP

Acacia brevispica (Prickly Acacia)
Acacia drepanolobium (Whistling Thorn)
Acacia gerrardii (Red Thorn/Grey-haired Acacia)
Acacia hockii
Acacia kirkii (Flood-plain Acacia)
Acacia mellifera (Black Thorn)
Acacia nilotica (Sweet Thorn)
Acacia polyacantha (White River Thorn)
Acacia robusta subsp. usambarensis, formerly
Acacia clavigera (Splendid Acacia or Stinking Acacia)
Acacia senegal (Three-thorned Acacia)
Acacia seyal (White Thorn)
Acacia sieberiana (Paper-bark Acacia)
Acacia tortilis (Umbrella Thorn)
Acacia xanthophloea (Fever Tree)
Faedherbia albida, Formerly *Acacia albida* (Ana Tree)

Most common Acacia associate

Commiphora trothae (Common Commiphora)

Kopje (rocky outcrop) trees and bushes

Acacia tortilis (Umbrella Thorn)
Albizia harveyi (Sickle-leaved Albizia)
Allophylus rubifolius (African Allophylus)
Capparis tomentosa (Wild Caper Bush)
Commiphora eminii
Commiphora merkeri (Zebra-bark Commiphora)
Commiphora trothae (Common Commiphora)
Cordia ovalis (Sandpaper Bush)
Dichrostachys cinerea (Sickle Bush)
Euphorbia bussei (Tree Euphorbia)
Euphorbia candelabrum (Candelabrum Tree)
Ficus thonningii (Strangler Fig)
Grewia fallax (Kopje Raison Bush)
Grewia trichocarpa (Wild Raison Bush)
Gymnosporia senegalensis (Confetti Tree)
Hibiscus lunarifolius (Kopje Hibiscus)
Lannea stuhlmannii (False Marula)
Maerua triphulla (Small Bead-bean)
Pavetta assimilis (Common Bride's Bush)
Phyllanthus sepialis (Dwarf Potato Bush)
Sclerocarya birrea (Marula Tree)
Teclea simplicifolia (Kopje Honeysuckle)
Turraea fischeri (Honeysuckle Tree)

Wooded Grassland

Balanites aegyptiaca (Green Thorn)

INTERESTING FACTS AND USES

The tree that visitors usually notice first when visiting the Serengeti is the flat-topped **Umbrella Thorn (*Acacia tortilis*).** The Umbrella Thorn Tree is one of the only woody species that occurs on the Short Grass Plains since its roots, unlike those of other trees, have the ability to penetrate the 'hard pan'- the solidified top

Umbrella Thorn Tree (Acacia tortilis)

layer of the soil. The pods are high in protein and relished by all browsers and primates. The flowers are eaten by Baboons and Monkeys. Elephants prefer the bark of the Umbrella Thorn but often destroy the tree in the de-barking process. The boiled root and bark yields a yellow-brown dye which is often used in basketry. It yields an edible gum of superior quality, which is one of the reasons why the Bushbaby *(Galago senegalensis)* favours this tree as a nesting site. Gum is an important part of the Bushbaby's diet. This animal demonstrates interesting behaviour in that it urinates on its hands and feet as part of social interaction and also to ensure a steadfast grip when executing huge leaps - up to 7m in one jump.

Lesser Bushbaby

Another *Acacia* that immediately catches the eye is the yellow-barked **Fever Tree (*Acacia xanthophloea*)** which grows along the rivers. It is called the Fever Tree because the early pioneers (during the middle 1800s), suspected it of causing malaria.

The truth is that it grows in the same low-lying, riverine areas that mosquitoes frequent - the female mosquito being the carrier of the malaria parasite, *Trypanosoma* spp. The wood is hard and useful but should be seasoned properly as it tends to crack easily. The Fever Tree grows fast and makes a very attractive ornamental garden tree. It is favoured by Buffalo Weavers, which build large communal nests, as the thorns probably provide protection from snakes and avian predators.

Fever Tree (Acacia xanthophloea)

The **Sausage Tree (*Kigelia africana*)** often occurs along rivers and grassland edges - in Seronera it is common along the edges of the plains. It is very attractive when in flower and in fruit. It bears cup-shaped, red flowers that are mainly pollinated by Fruit Bats, and which have a very strong, rather unpleasant smell. It has huge, sausage-shaped fruits of up to 1m long. Baboons and Hippos eat the fruit and Giraffe chew the young fruit like a huge piece of chewing gum. The pips of the fruit are used in Zimbabwe to produce a commercial skin cancer prevention lotion. Many of the superstitions and medicinal uses of the fruits of this tree relate to impotency cures and aphrodisiacs, no doubt in direct reference to their shape.

Sausage Tree (Kigelia africana)

Swollen gall of the Whistling Thorn

Whistling Thorn (Acacia depranolobium)

Another unique tree is the **Whistling Thorn (*Acacia depranolobium*)**, which has swollen, black galls at the base of the larger spines. The galls are hollow and are inhabited by a small species of stinging ant. One can recognise the ants by the way that they hold their abdomens straight up, but beware, they have quite a painful sting. Scattered along the tree are numerous extra-floral nectaries which resemble flowers, on which the stinging ants feed. This is an example of a symbiotic relationship between plants and insects, where the plant offers a living environment and food to the ants whilst they protect it from severe browsing by attacking the browsers if they feed for too long on the same tree. The galls are hollow, having holes where the ants can enter. These holes produce a whistling sound when the wind blows through them - hence the common name of 'Whistling Thorn'.

Another interesting *Acacia* is the **Robust Thorn** or **Stinking Acacia (*A. robusta*)** which is common along hillsides and does not have particularly nasty thorns to defend itself against browsers. It does, however, produce an unpleasant chemical in its bark and wood that deters browsers, earning it the common name of 'Stinking Acacia'.

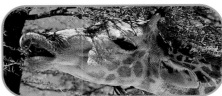

Giraffe browsing on an Acacia tree

One of the most common trees on tall grassland is the **Green Thorn (*Balanites aegyptiaca*)** with its distinctly half-moon canopy, green, drooping branches and large green thorns scattered evenly along the branches. The significance of the green colour of the thorns is that they contain chlorophyll, which enables the tree to photosynthesise even when it is devoid of leaves. The leaves are paired and the thorns simple. The fruits are not poisonous to man and are used medicinally to treat spleen and liver complaints. However, the fruit is very

poisonous to aquatic fauna and small fish but does not affect air-breathing aquatic fauna such as mosquito larvae and pupae. It is very effective against snails and the intermediate host of the fluke, *Schistosomiasis sp.*, which causes Bilharzia. It is used extensively in the Sudan to control Bilharzia.

Green Thorn (Balanites aegyptiaca)

Bilhazia parasite (Plasmodium vivax)

The toxicity takes effect as soon as the mashed fruit is placed in water. One fruit in 30 litres of water is enough to kill snails. It can be used in controlling garden snails as well. The fruits are not poisonous to man but they are very bitter, and are therefore seldom eaten. The mashed bark is very effective as fish poison. Many tribes in Africa employ this method to kill fish for human consumption as the meat does not become contaminated in the process. Many plants that are used as fish poison contain a toxic crystalline substance known as rotenone, the main ingredient in derris insecticides.

V E G E T A T I O N - T R E E S

Derris is a poison that was originally obtained from a leguminous plant discovered in the East Indies. Fish are extremely susceptible to rotenone poisoning and the effect is one of paralysis of the nervous system, preceded by convulsions. This means that toxic compounds travel via the nerves and not via the blood or lymphatic system. If that was the case, the meat of the fish would be contaminated. Death therefore results from respiratory paralysis, which renders the meat harmless. As the fish die, they float to the surface and are collected in baskets.

The bark of the Green Thorn is used as fish poison

The **Marula Tree (*Sclerocarya birrea*)** is not very common in the Serengeti but it produces tasty fruit that the animals relish. The fruit can be used to produce a jelly or an alcoholic beverage. The kernels are very high in oil content and currently tests are being done to produce a sunblock from the oil. Marula fruits contain four times more Vitamin C than orange juice.

Maruala Tree (Sclerocarya birrea)

Date Palm (Phoenix reclinata)

Another tree that must be mentioned here is the **Date Palm (*Phoenix reclinata*)** which bears edible fruit that resemble dates in taste. The sap of the tree can also be tapped to produce a very refreshing alcoholic beverage if left to ferment. The Palm Swift often builds its nest from mud on the leaves of Date Palms. They use saliva to glue the eggs to the nest and they actually brood the eggs vertically.

Whistling Thorn (Acacia depranolobium)

*Whistling Thorn
(Acacia depranolobium)*

**Prickly Acacia
(Acacia brevispica)**

Flood-plain Acacia (Acacia kirkii)

*Flood-plain Acacia
(Acacia kirkii)*

*Flood-plain Acacia
(Acacia kirkii)*

Black Thorn (Acacia mellifera)

*Black Thorn
(Acacia mellifera)*

*Black Thorn
(Acacia mellifera)*

Scented Thorn (Acacia nilotica)

Scented Thorn (Acacia nilotica)

VEGETATION - TREES

67

White River Thorn
(Acacia polyacantha)

White River Thorn
(Acacia polyacantha)

Three-thorned Acacia
(Acacia senegal)

Three-thorned Acacia
(Acacia senegal)

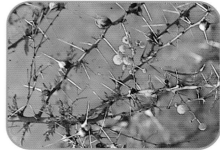

White Thorn
(Acacia seyal)

White Thorn
(Acacia seyal)

Paper-bark Acacia
(Acacia sieberiana)

Paper-bark Acacia
(Acacia sieberiana)

Umbrella Thorn
(Acacia tortilis)

Umbrella Thorn
(Acacia tortilis)

Fever Tree
(Acacia xanthophloea)

Green Thorn/Single thorned Torchwood
(Balanites aegyptiaca)

Small-leaved Shepherd's Tree
(Boscia angustifolia)

Cassia
(Cassia didymobotrys)

Wild Caper Bush
(Capparis tomentosa)

Wild Caper Bush
(Capparis tomentosa)

VEGETATION - TREES

Carissa or Num-num
(Carissa edulis)

Carissa or Num-num
(Carissa edulis)

Carissa or Num-num
(Carissa edulis)

Acacia Bushland Commiphora
(Commiphora trothae)

Acacia Bushland Commiphora
(Commiphora trothae)

Sandpaper Bush
(Cordia ovalis)

Sandpaper Bush
(Cordia ovalis)

Sickle Bush
(Dichrostachys cinerea)

Sickle Bush
(Dichrostachys cinerea)

Sickle Bush
(Dichrostachys cinerea)

VEGETATION – TREES

Candelabra Tree
(Euphorbia candelabrum)

Tree Euphorbia
(Euphorbia bussei)

Rock Fig
(Ficus lutea)

Rock Fig
(Ficus lutea)

Sycamore Fig
(Ficus sycomorus)

Sycamore Fig
(Ficus sycomorus)

Strangler Fig
(Ficus thonningii)

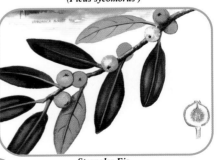

Strangler Fig
(Ficus thonningii)

African Mangosteen
(Garcinia livingstonei)

African Mangosteen
(Garcinia livingstonei)

Gardenia
(Gardenia volkensii)

Gardenia
(Gardenia volkensii)

Raisin Bush
(Grewia bicolor)

Raisin Bush
(Grewia bicolor)

Giant Raisin Bush
(Grewia tenuinervis)

Giant Raisin Bush
(Grewia tenuinervis)

VEGETATION - TREES

Confetti Tree
(Gymnosporia senegalensis)

Kopje Hibiscus
(Hibiscus lunariifolius)

Sausage Tree
(Kigelia africana)

Sausage Tree
(Kigelia africana)

Broad-leafed Lance-pod
(Lonchocarpus eriocalyx)

Broad-leafed Lance-pod
(Lonchocarpus eriocalyx)

Indaba Tree
(Pappaea capensis)

Poison Apple
(Solanum sp.)

73

Date Palm
(Phoenix reclinata)

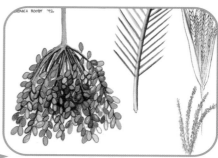

Date Palm
(Phoenix reclinata)

Marula Tree
(Sclerocarya birrea)

Marula Tree
(Sclerocarya birrea)

Honeysuckle Tree
(Turraea robusta)

Honeysuckle Tree
(Turraea robusta)

Umbrella Thorn Tree (Acacia tortilis)

INTERESTING FACTS AND USES

The **Devil's Horsewhip (*Achyranthus aspera*)** is an erect herb with slightly drooping spikes and tiny, star-shaped flowers. An extraction of the plant is said to increase heart rate and urine output. The leaf ash is applied to boils, abscesses, sores and the root is chewed for toothache. The ash is used as a substitute for salt and, mixed with tobacco, produces a very potent snuff. The ash froths when mixed

with water, making it suitable as a soap to wash clothes. The plant produces a very good pot-ash which is used to soften and flavour meat and traditional foods.

Devil's Horsewhip (Achyranthus aspera)

The Milkweed (*Asclepias fruticosa*) is easily recognised by its sharply-pointed, golf-ball sized fruit covered in purplish bristles. The plant is toxic but in small doses is used medicinally. Infusions of all plant parts are effective against stomach complaints, diarrhoea and coughs. It irritates the intestinal wall and stimulates intestinal movement, making it a good substitute for Senna (a yellow-flowered tropical plant traditionally used for stomach complaints). The latex is applied directly to warts to make them disappear. The bark is very strong and can be used as string. The crushed plant is stuffed into mole holes to deter them. The silky seed threads are used to stuff mattresses. The high cellulose content (82%) in the seed thread makes for an excellent tinder because it causes an

instant energy release. Early Europeam settlers used it in tinderbox lamps and as a substitute for guncotton, mixing it with gunpowder to load cartridges.

Milkweed (Asclepias fruticosa)

The African Monarch Butterfly (*Danaus chrysippus*) is closely associated with this plant as the larvae feed on it. The butterfly and the larva are thus poisonous and ignored by most insect predators. Other butterflies mimic the Monarch to render them safe against predation. One such species is the female Common Diadem (*Hypolimnas misippus*), which is actually quite palatable. The male of this

species looks like a completely different species. The Milkweed is very similar to *Gomphocarpus physocarpa* but the fruits of the latter are more rounded.

The African Monarch (Danaus chrysippus)

The **Climbing Cactus**, also known as the **Edible-stemmed Vine** or **Four-angled Vine (*Cissus quadrangularis*)** is a common vine on kopjes and has edible stems. The fresh leaves and powdered stems are applied to burns and wounds and are said to be effective treatments for saddle sores on horses. A extraction of the stems and leaf is administered orally for gastro-intestinal complaints and to induce milk yield in cattle. A potent anabolic steroid

has been isolated from this plant, and has proved most effective in bone fracture healing, inducing early regeneration and quicker mineralisation (Hutchings et. al, 1996).

Climbing Cactus (Cisuss quadrangularis)

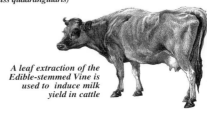

A leaf extraction of the Edible-stemmed Vine is used to induce milk yield in cattle

The flowers of the purplish-blue **Wandering Jew (*Commelina benguallensis*)** resemble a tiny mouse face with the petals as ears and the spathe as a nose. Mucilage from the flowering parts is used to treat thrush in infants. Bruised leaves are applied to external wounds and to treat burns. The plant juice is taken orally against sore throats and, mixed with water, is used to bathe sore eyes. The plant juice is said to be an astringent, reducing blood flow in external wounds. It is also used to treat diarrhoea and dysentry. *Commelina petersii* is similar to the *C. benguallensis*, but the flowers are larger (±2,5cm). *Commelina africana* has yellow flowers and *C. reptans* has orange flowers.

Commelina benguallensis   *Commelina reptans*

The **Crotalarias (*Crotalaria sp.*)** have yellow, pea-like flowers and usually three leaflets. They are known to be poisonous and most species in the genus affect the liver, lungs and kidneys. Hepatotoxic (liver poison) alkaloids have been isolated in almost all species. The alkaloids in *Crotalaria* are responsible for the peculiar growth disturbance in hooves often observed in domestic stock. They cause inflammation of the internal parts of the hooves. At first the animal walks stiffly and the hooves are warm, after which the hooves grow out and curl up. The toxin can also occlude (block) the bronchi in the lungs and cause animals to show symptoms of bronchitis.

Crotalaria volkensii   *The growth disturbance caused in hooves by Crotalaria poisoning*

The **Pink Ink Flower (*Cycnium tubulosum ssp. montanum*)** is one of the most common and noticeable ground covers or low-growing herbs in the SNP, preferring heavy, clayey soils. It grows mainly in black cotton soils and is a semi-parasite, obtaining some of their nutrients from grass roots. The leaves are linear-lanceolate, often toothed, and the flowers are large (4cm to 5cm), bright pink with yellow centres. They are called 'Ink Flowers' because they turn bluish with age, not because they produce ink. An extraction of this plant is often used as an emetic love charm.

Pink Ink Flower (Cycnium tubulosun)

The **White Ink Flower (*Cycnium tubulosum ssp. tubulosum*)** is the white version (sub-species) of the Pink Ink Flower, and usually grows alongside it.

White Ink Flower (Cycnium tubulosun)

The **Flame Lily (*Gloriosa superba*)** is a striking plant with five upward curving, red and yellow petals, resembling flames. It is extremely poisonous, but the corm, which is more poisonous than the leaves and flowers, is eaten by porcupines without ill effect. The powdered corm is used all over Africa as an aphrodisiac. It is also administered to infertile women to induce ovulation, but studies have shown that its administration can result in deformed babies. The plant contains the highly toxic alkaloid, colchicine, a well-known commercial gout medicine. The corm is used externally as a disinfectant to treat wounds, haemorrhoids, skin diseases and toothache. A root infusion is taken against worms. A sap derived from the root is used very effectively to poison vermin. It is so poisonous that a small dosage is enough to kill a dog. The corm of this plant takes on a peculiar, gnarled shape and is often used in rites where a child of a certain gender is preferred. A pregnant mother is given an infusion made from the corm that resembles the required gender but, as was pointed out above, this often leads to deformed babies.

The Flame Lily (Gloriosa superba)

The **Wild Stockrose (*Hibiscus calyphyllus*)** is a low shrub of ±50cm with simple or three-lobed, circular leaves and flowers with maroon centres. The flowers can be cooked as a vegetable but are generally only used during times of famine. A baby with a sunken fontanelle is treated with a powdered root mixture of this plant. The larva of the largest of the Hawk Moths (*Laphostethus dumolini*) feeds on this genus, as does the caterpillar of the Spiny Bollworm moth (*Earuas biplaga*). As cotton plants are also part of this family, these caterpillars can cause severe economic damage to cotton fields.

Wild Stockrose (Hibiscuc calyphyllus)

Arrow Sphinx (Lophosthethus dumolini)

The flowers of the **Jute Fibre Hibiscus (*Hibiscus cannabinus*)**, can be yellow with maroon centres or they can be a beautiful mauvy-purple colour. The leaves are five- to seven-lobed and the flowers droop, especially in the late afternoon. In India this plant is very important as it is the source of hemp or jute fibre. The fibre is extracted by means of retting (the anaerobic under-water rotting of stems with the help of the bacterium *Clostridium felsinae*). The seed has a high oil content and is suitable for soap-making.

Jute Fibre Hibiscus (Hibiscus cannabinus)

The **Indigophora Herb (*Indigophora hochstetteri*)** belongs to a genus that usually has compound leaves and pea-shaped flowers, often blue, pink or purple in colour. A blue dye (indigo) is obtained from a number of tropical species in this genus. Indigo is very poisonous and can be used to cause vomiting or to treat diarrhoea and muscular spasms.

Indigophora Herb (Indigophora hochstetteri)

The **Leafy-bract Justicaea (*Justicea betonica*)** is the host plant of the Gaika Blue Butterfly (*Zizula hylax hylax*).

Leafy-bract Justicea (Justicea betonica)

The succulent **Kalanchoe (*Kalanchoe lanceolata*)** is erect with attractive orange flowers and paired, boat-shaped leaves. When mixed with snuff, the ground plant induces severe sneezing, which is said to clear the head during a cold. The powdered root is applied to the nose during colds to prevent cold sores.

Kalanchoe (Kalanchoe lanceeolata)

The **Lion's Paw (*Leonotis nepetifolia*)** is an erect, down-covered plant with paired, drooping leaves borne below the globose, red-flowered flowerheads that occur at intervals along the stem. The dried leaves are smoked in southern Africa, but does not have any hallucinogenic properties. An extraction of the plant, mixed with saltpetre, is used to treat syphilitic ulcers and, mixed with pumpkin seeds, it is taken orally to treat tapeworm. This species occurs at lower altitudes on the plains but also occurs on the highlands up to 2 000m above sea level.

Lion's Paw
(*Leonotis nepetifolia*)

The **Bushmen's Tea or Fever Bush (*Lippia javanica*)** is commercially marketed in Botswana as a herbal tea with medicinal properties. It is widely used for treating coughs, colds, bronchial ailments and fever. It is also used as an eye-wash for sore eyes. The smoke from the burnt leaves is used to clear the chest. The leaves are highly aromatic and when burnt, are an effective insect repellent.

Bushman's Tea
(*Lippia javanica*)

The **Blue Pentanysia (*Pentanysia ouranogyne*)** is a low-growing herb with linear to lanceolate leaves. It has very attractive, blue flowers arranged in roundish, terminal bunches or corymbs. The flowers are about 6mm across. It is common in the Serengeti and thrives in dry areas in disturbed soil, often next to roads. The root of the plant is used as a laxative and to treat abdominal pains.

Blue Pentanysia
(*Pentanysia ouranogyne*)

The **Tattoo Plant (*Plumbago zeylanica*)** is a perennial climber with white, tubular flowers with a green calyx covered in sticky hairs. It is widely used in Africa for cosmetic tattooing by tying the fresh, de-barked root closely to the skin and leaving it for 24 hours. A blister will form and after the skin is removed, the skin will darken. The root contains 4% plumbagin, a chemical that stimulates smooth muscles and the central nervous system. Root scrapings are pushed directly into the uterus to induce abortion. This plant also dilates peripheral blood vessels, causing blood pressure to lower. Large doses result in paralysis. The root is also used to treat hookworm in cattle, scabies, skin infections and yaws. The root juice is applied externally to the penis as a very painful treatment for sexually transmitted diseases. The plant juice is applied directly to infected eyes of cattle and the bruised root is fed to livestock to induce ovulation.

Blue Pentanysia
(*Pentanysia ouranogyne*)

The **Fireball Lily or Royal Shaving Brush (*Scadoxus multiflorus*)** has bright red flowers borne on a single stem on large, round flowerheads. It is very attractive and appears just before the first rains. It occurs in rocky areas, riverine forest, grassland, often in the shade of trees and at the edges of termite heaps. It grows from a bulb that is quite deep beneath the surface. It occurs from sea level to 2 700m. It is not very common but can be seen virtually in any vegetation type. The plant is poisonous but, like many poisonous plants, is also used as a medicine. The bulb juice is used to treat external wounds and scabies. It is also taken orally for colds and asthma. The slimy juice is applied to the groin and vagina of a cow to induce birth. By applying the juice

directly to a cow's udder, milk yield can be improved. The macerated bulb is used as fish poison and, mixed with other plants, is used as arrow poison.

Fireball Lily
(Scadoxus multiflorus)

The **Sodom Apple (*Solanum incanum*)** belongs to a genus that has blue, star-shaped flowers with yellow stamens in the middle, arranged like a pyramid. There are prickles scattered along the stems and stalks and the leaves are ovate to lanceolate. A root extraction is taken orally for chest complaints and

haemorrhoids. The fruit is poisonous when green but it is administered orally and externally to animals to treat ringworm, a skin disease caused by a fungus. The root is chewed for toothache and to treat stomach pains and indigestion.

Sodom Apple
(Solanum incanum)

The **Witchweed (*Striga asiatica*)** is a root

parasite that grows mainly on maize, sorghum and sugarcane but does occur in damp areas in the Serengeti where it parasitises grasses. The leaves are linear (narrow) and the flowers a bright red (±1,5cm), borne in terminal spikes.

Witchweed
(Striga asaitica)

The **Khaki weed (*Tagetes minuta*)** is an erect, strong-smelling weed with small, cream-yellow flowers borne at the top of the plant. It is very common in disturbed places at altitudes from 700m to 2 200m. It originates in America and is said to have been introduced during World War I in horse fodder by the British who were referred to by the Boers in South Africa as the 'Khakis' - hence the common name.

Khaki Weed
(Tagetes minuta)

The **Tortoise Food Bush (*Talinum caffrum*)** is a small herb with succulent leaves and star-shaped, yellow flowers. The leaves can be eaten fresh but they become soapy and slimy when chewed - very effective to treat severe thirst. Tortoises relish the thick leaves. A root infusion can be taken orally or as an enema to treat abdominal complaints. In the Kalahari desert the slimy leaf juice is commonly used for 'bathing' by smearing the body with the crushed leaves.

Leopard Tortoise

Tortoise Food Bush
(Talinum caffrum)

The **Devil's Thorn (*Tribulus terestris*)** is a much-branched, prostrate herb with compound leaves and attractive yellow, five-petalled flowers. It is associated with disturbed soils where it covers vast areas and is most common along roadsides. It produces spiny, woody burrs which attach to shoes or hooves - a very effective form or seed dispersal. Some tribes use these thorns as an initiation test. An area is covered with the thorns and the young men are made to walk over it barefoot without showing any outward sign of pain.

Devil's Thorn (Tribulus terestris)

The **Cornflower-blue Vernonia (*Vernonia glabra*)** is an erect plant with large, leathery, grey-green leaves with serrated edges. The flowers are blue and composite. This plant is widely used as an abortion plant by inserting the root directly into the uterus. It is also used to induce menstruation, to reduce menstrual pains and to treat gonorrhoea. The root is effective for stomach problems and the leaf ash is used as an antiseptic for burns. It attracts many butterflies, one of the most common being the Brown-veined White (*Belenois aurota aurota*).

Cornflower-blue Vernonia (Vernonia glabra)

Blue Water Lily (Nymphaea nouchali var. caerulea)

Photographic wild flower check list - green

Khaki Burweed
(Alternanthera pungens)

Milkweed / Wild Cotton
(Asclepias fruticosa)

Wild Asparagus
(Asparagus sp.)

Edible-stemmed Vine
(Cissus quadrangularis)

Cissampelos
(Cissampelos mucronata)

Giant Sedge
(Cyperus giganteum)

Wild Grape
(Cyphostemma nierienses)

Bachelor's Button
(Gomphrena celosioides)

Wild Basil
(Ocimum sp.)

Buffalo-horn Climber
(Pergularia daemia)

Dwarf Potato Bush
(Phyllanthus sp.)

Wild Asparagus
(Protasparagus sp.)

Mother-in-law's tongue
(Sansevieria ehrenbergiana)

Mother-in-law's tongue
(Sansevieria sp.)

Black Night-shade
(Solanum nigrum)

Khaki Weed
(Tagetes minuta)

VEGETATION - WILD FLOWERS

Photographic wild flower check list - white

Anthericum)
(Anthericum sp.)

Large Morning Glory
(Astripomoea hyoscyamoides)

Barleria
(Barleria ventricosa)

Carissa / Num-num
(Carissa edulis)

Clematis
(Clematis brachiata)

Clerodendrum
(Clerodendrum sp.)

Doll's Plumbago
(Commicarpus plumbagineus)

Cyathula
(Cyathula polycephala)

Sedge
(Cyperus obtusiflorus)

White Ink Flower
(Cycnium tubulosum
subsp. tubulosum)

Larkspur
(Delphinium leroyi)

Geranium
(Geranium arabicum)

Spider Wisp
(Gynandropis gynandra)

Scorpion Flower
(Heliotropium steudneri)

Hibiscus
(Hibiscus flavifolius)

Hibiscus
(Hibiscus fuscus)

Photographic wild flower check list - white continued

Giant Morning Glory
(Ipomoea kituensis)

Long-tubed Morning Glory
(Ipomoea longituba)

Ground-creeper Morning Glory *(Ipomoea mombassana)*

Purple-throated Ipomoea
(Ipomoea sinensis)

Wild Jasmine
(Jasminum fluminense)

Dainty Justicea
(Justica anselliana)

Leafy-bract Justica
(Justicea betonica)

Bushman's Tea
(Lippia javanica)

Leucas
(Leucas deflexa)

Blue Water Lily (Nymphaea nouchali var. caerulea)

Lotis Lily
(Nymphaea lotus)

Ornithogalum Lily
(Ornithogalum cameronii)

Spider Lily
(Pancratium tenuifolium)

Pavetta
(Pavetta spp.)

Tattoo Plant
(Plumbago zeylarica)

Ruellia
(Ruellia patula)

VEGETATION - WILD FLOWERS

83

Photographic wild flower check list - yellow

Toilet Paper Bush /
Elephant's Ear
(Abutilon angulatum)

Abutilon
(Abutilon mauritianum)

Swamp Weed
(Aeschynomene indica)

Wild Marigold
(Aspilia mossambicensis)

Leopard Orchid
(Ansellia africana)

Leopard Orchid Flower
(Ansellia africana)

Wild Marigold
(Bidens taitensis)

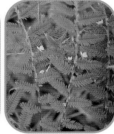

Dwarf Cassia
(Cassia hilldebrandtii)

Yellow Spider Wisp
(Cleome angustifolia)

Giant Crotalaria
(Crotalaria laburnifolia)

Crotalaria
(Crotalaria sp.)

Crotalaria
(Crotalaria volkensii)

Grassland Orchard
(Eulophia welwitchii)

Everlasting Flowers
(Helichrysum sp.)

Wild Stockrose
(Hibiscus calyphyllus)

Wild Hemp
(Hibiscus cannabinus)

Photographic wild flower check list - yellow continued

Hirpicium
(Hirpicium diffusum)

Ipomoea
(Ipomoea obscura)

Yellow Justicea
(Justicea flava)

Bushman's Tea
(Lippia javanica)

Ludwigia
(Ludwigia stolonifera)

Snuff Plant
(Kalanchoe lanceolata)

Honeycup
(Melhania ovata)

Honeycup
(Melhania sp.)

Ottelia / Water-pistol
(Ottelia ulvifolia)

Pavonia
(Pavonia gallaensis)

Pavonia
(Pavonia senegalensis)

Wild Purslane
(Portulaca grandiflora)

Tortoise Food
(Talinum caffrum)

Sesbania
(Sesbania bispinosa)

Black-eyed Susan
(Thunbergia alata)

Devil's Thorn
(Tribilus terestris)

VEGETATION - WILD FLOWERS

Photographic wild flower check list - pink / purple

VEGETATION - WILD FLOWERS

Devil's Horsewhip
(Achyranthus aspera)

Barleria
(Barleria argentea)

Blepharis
(Blepharis hildebrandtii)

Bothriocline
(Bothriocline tomentosum)

Commelina
(Commelina benguallensis)

Pink Commicarpus
(Commicarpus pudunculosus)

Resurection Plant
(Craterostigma plantagineum)

Resurection Plant
(Craterostigma pumilum)

Crinum Lily
(Crinum macowani)

Purple Crotalaria
(Crotalaria sp.)

Cynoglossum
(Cynoglossum coeruleum)

Pink Ink Flower (Cycnium
tubulosum ssp. montuosum)

Ink Flower
(Cycnium sp.)

Cystostemon
(Cystostemon hispidum)

Thorn Apple
(Datura stramonium)

Evolvulus
(Evolvulus alsinoides)

(Floscopa)
Floscopa glomerata

Gutenbergia
(Gutenbergia cordifolia)

Jute Fibre
(Hibiscus cannabinus)

Indigophora
(Indigophora sp.)

Common Morning Glory
(Ipomoea jaegeri)

Morning Glory
(Ipomoea wightii)

Lantana
(Lantana camara)

Blue Water Lily
(Nymphaea nouchali var. caerulea)

Pentanisia
(Pentanisia ouranogyn)

Ruellia
(Ruellia patula)

Wild Sesame
(Sesamum angustifolium)

Poison Apple
(Solamum incanum)

Purple Witchweed
(Striga gesneroides)

Tephrosia
(Tephrosia purpurea)

Cornflower-blue Vernonia
(Vernonia glabra)

Wild Bean
(Vigna membranacea)

VEGETATION - WILD FLOWERS

Photographic wild flower check list - red / orange

Aloe
(Aloe sp.)

Aloe
(Aloe secundiflora)

Aloe
(Aloe volkensii)

Orange Commelina
(Commelina reptans)

Crossandra
(Crossandra nilotica)

Emilia
(Emilia coccinea)

Gladiolus / Parot Beak
(Gladiolus natalensis)

Flame Lily
(Gloriosa superba)

Scarlet Hibiscus
(Hibiscus aponeurus)

Snuff Plant
(Kalanchoe lanceolata)

Sausage Tree
(Kigelia africana)

Lion's Paw
(Leonotis nepetifolia)

Red Hot Poker
(Kniphofia thomsonii)

Red Hot Poker
(Kniphofia thomsonii)

Fire-ball Lily
(Scadoxus multiforus)

Witchweed
(Striga asaitica)

VEGETATION - WILD FLOWERS

COMMON GRASSES

INTERESTING FACTS AND USES

Blue Buffalo Grass (*Cenchrus ciliaris*) prefers sandy and limy soils and is an indicator of healthy veld conditions where it often forms climax communities. It also flourishes in deserted stock pens. It is high in fodder value but becomes fibrous with age, especially in under-utilised veld. It can be identified by the spiky flowerheads

and the bluish tinge to the leaves. It has a root system of over 2m deep and is very effective for soil binding. An extraction of the rhizomes are used for menstrual and urinary disorders in women.

Blue Buffalo Grass (Cenchrus ciliaris)

Couch Grass (*Cynodon dactylon*) has a digitate (finger-like) flowerhead and grows ±30cm high. It is an indicator of saline soils and tends to take over where there is mild over-grazing. It often grows near salt lakes and has a vigorous rhizome system which enables it to form large stands and which makes it very effective in erosion control. It is not as high in nutrition as Red Oat Grass (*Themeda triandra*) but it has a very high yield and does not become woody. The more it is grazed, the more it grows, making it ideal as a lawn grass. An extraction of the rhizome is used as a blood purifier, to cause urination and to bring down swelling. It is also effective against heartburn and to treat external wounds. When it wilts, it can cause

bloat in animals because of the large concentrations of prussic acid that build up. The larva of the common Evening Brown Butterfly (*Melanitis leda*) feeds on this grass.

Couch Grass (Cynodon dactylon)

Rhodes' Grass (*Chloris gayana*) prefers well-drained, moist soils and is an indicator of stable conditions. It can be recognised by the digitate (finger-like) flowerheads with their red-brown colour. It is a highly valued forage grass and various strains are being cultivated worldwide. It is also very effective in erosion control, especially in damp areas such as dam walls. The grass was named after Cecil John Rhodes (1853-1902), who introduced the grass to South Africa in 1895 from India, specifically for its nutritious value.

Rhodes' Grass (Chloris gayana)

Feather-top Chloris (*Chloris virgata*) can be recognised by its white, feathery spikes, arranged in whorls. It is a pioneer grass, in other words it grows in denuded areas and is an indicator of overgrazing and disturbance. It prefers moist, clayey soils that are slightly saline. It is low in nutrition but is readily grazed when young. The steam from the boiled roots is inhaled to cure colds. Weaver birds use the flowerheads to line their nests.

Feather-top Chloris (Chloris virgata)

Weaver Birds use the soft flowerheads of the Feather-top Chloris to line their nests

Turpentine Grass (*Cymbopogon excavatus*) has a very strong, turpentine smell which deters grazers, although it is quite high in nutrition It becomes woody and even more unpalatable at maturity. It prefers stony or damp areas. It is one of the most sought-after thatching grasses. It yields an essential oil related to citronella oil, a well-known insect repellent. The smoke from the burnt flower-heads is very effective for this purpose. It is also used to line grain baskets, to deter rodents.

Turpentine Grass
(Cymbopogon excavatus)

Crow's Foot Grass (*Dactyloctenium aegyptium*) can be recognised by its 'crow's foot' flowerhead. It is low in fodder value and an indicator of disturbed soils.

Crow's Foot Grass
(Dactyloctenium aegyptium)

Goose Grass (*Eleusine coracana*) was formerly known as *E. indica*. It is a short grass of ±30cm with a vigorous root system that becomes a hardy weed in cultivated lands. It is fairly palatable when young but becomes tough with age and is an indicator of overgrazing and veld disturbance. The plant can be cultivated to obtain a kind of millet. It is used for a variety of medi inal applications - the juice is given to women to relieve pain in childbirth, it is used to treat chest conditions, dysentery, to counteract dandruff, as an eye wash, and to induce vomiting and urinating. It is also widely used to treat worms, especially *Ascaris*, a nematode that has man and pigs as hosts.

Goose Grass
(Eleusine coracana)

Spear Grass (*Heteropogon contortus*) has a high feeding value in the wet season but low in the dry season. It tends to take over where there is moderate grazing and is ignored mostly because of the harmful nature of the awns (long hair-like growths on the flower-head) which form tangled masses. The awns are spiralled and when they come into contact with water, they de-spiral and dig into the soil. This species prefers well-drained and stony soils.

Spear Grass
(Heteropogon contortus)

Thatching Grass (*Hyparrhenia rufa*) occurs in moist soils and can be seen near swampy areas. It has rusty-brown, paired racemes (spikes) and grows up to 2,5 m high. It is a valuable fodder grass early in the rainy season but as soon as it becomes woody, it is ignored. It is commonly used as a thatching grass. It is an indicator of under-utilisation where it tends to form climax communities.

Thatching Grass
(Hyparrhenia rufa)

Buffalo Grass (*Panicum maximum*) is probably the grass with the highest protein value (10,4% in the wet season and 8,7% in the dry season), but it fails to form large stands. It favours heavy, nitrogen-rich soils and favours to grow in shade, often under *Acacia* or other pod-bearing plants. Its presence is an indication that the veld is in very good condition. Its flowerhead has a christmas tree shape (panicle). It is one of the first to disappear under grazing pressure.

Buffalo Grass
(Panicum maximum)

VEGETATION - GRASSES

Around the pans, the most saline resistant of all is ***Odyssea* sp.**, which grows closest to the pans. It grows from rhizomes and is important in erosion control around salty pans. It is a very unfriendly grass with sharply-pointed, rigid leaves.

*Salt Grass
(Odyssea sp.)*

Common Reed (*Phragmites mauritianus*) grows about 5m tall and is found along water courses. The young shoots are eaten by Elephants, Reedbuck and the Canerat. Even Elephants ignore mature reeds but they do churn them up to get to the rhizomes. Reeds are important as building material and in basketry. It offers refuge to Canerats, Weavers, Widow Birds, Whydas and Finches. The Thick-billed Weavers often construct their nests between two reeds. The female Carpenter bee bores into the reeds for laying her eggs. She collects pollen and nectar which are carefully deposited into a cell with a single egg, which is then closed. Several cells are constructed next to each other. This mixture of pollen, nectar and bees' eggs is sweet and tasty and often sought after by children.

*Common Reed
(Phragmites mauritianus)*

Bur-bristle Grass (*Setaria verticillata*) can be an irritating grass because of its bur-bristle flowerheads which attach themselves to anything and everything. It prefers to grow in the shade, invariably coinciding with the best camping spots. Not all is bad to be said about this grass, as it is a valuable fodder grass with high palatability, especially when young. It prefers nitrogen-rich soils in disturbed areas and is an indication of over-grazing. It has grave economic implications for sheep farmers, as the seeds devalue the wool. It can be used effectively to deter rodents and birds from stealing grain by simply covering the grain with a thick layer of flowerheads. The ash from this grass is used as cooking salt.

*Bur-bristle Grass
(Setaria verticillata)*

Wild Sorghum Grass (*Sorghum versicolor*) is a very tall species (2,5m to 3m) and has a typical christmas tree flowerhead. It is palatable and suitable for making hay. The seeds are sorghum-like and are used as food by various tribes. The ash from the plant is used as cooking salt. It grows in disturbed, damp places and never forms very large stands.

*Wild Sorghum Grass
(Sorghum versicolor)*

Pan Dropseed Grass (*Sporobolus iocladus*) is a palatable grass with a fairly high nutritive value. It is an indication of brackish soils and will decrease with grazing pressure. It has a christmas tree flowerhead and loses its seeds, like others in the genus. It retains its palatability during the dry season.

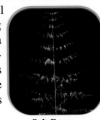

*Salt Grass
(Odyssea sp.)*

Pan Dropseed Grass usually grows near salt pans

Spike Grass or Spiky Dropseed (*Sporobolus spicatus*) is one of the more salt-resistant grasses, growing around salt lakes. It is called 'dropseed' because the seeds are dropped to the ground at maturity.

It can be recognised by its narrow spikes. The leaves are rigid and spiky - a very unfriendly grass. It is totally unpalatable but is a good indicator of saline soils and a handy soil binder around salt lakes where it tends to form climax communities. The leaves are rigid and sharply-pointed.

Spike Grass (Sporobolus spicatus)

The single most common grass species that occurs in the open tall-grass areas of the Serengeti National Park and elsewhere in East Africa, is **Red Oat Grass (*Themeda triandra*)**. It grows on all soil types and has a fairly good nutritive value. It is favoured by grazers in its young stage but when it becomes mature it is often ignored, especially by selective feeders. It is easy to recognise by the characteristic oat-like spikelets and the fact that the grass turns reddish-brown at maturity. It is extremely variable in habitat choice, growing in lowlands as well as in mountain grassland. Its presence is an indication of healthy, well-managed, climax veld where it forms large homogeneous communities.

Red Oat Grass (Themeda triandra)

Photographic grass check list

Pinhole Grass (Bothriachloa insculpta) ⟷ *Pinhole Grass (Bothriachloa insculpta)*

Blue Buffalo Grass (Cenchrus ciliaris) ⟷ *Blue Buffalo Grass (Cenchrus ciliaris)*

Rhodes Grass (Chloris gayana) ⟷ *Rhodes Grass (Chloris gayana)*

Feather-top Chloris (Chloris virgata) ⟷ *Feather-top Chloris (Chloris virgata)*

Photographic grass check list continued

Turpentine Grass
(Cymbopogon excavatus)
Turpentine Grass
(Cymbopogon excavatus)
Couch Grass
(Cynodon dactylon)
Couch Grass
(Cynodon dactylon)

Crow's Foot Grass
(Dactyloctenium aegyptium
Crow's Foot Grass
(Dactyloctenium aegyptium
Swamp Grass
(Diplachne fusca)
Swamp Grass
(Diplachne fusca)

Goose Grass
(Eleusine coracana)
Goose Grass
(Eleusine coracana)
Nine-awned Grass
(Enneapogon cenchroides)
Nine-awned Grass
(Enneapogon cenchroides)

Needle Grass
(Enteropogon macrostachyus)
Needle Grass
(Enteropogon macrostachyus)
Rough Love Grass
(Eragrostis aspera)
Rough Love Grass
(Eragrostis aspera)

VEGETATION - GRASSES

93

Photographic grass check list continued

Sticky Love Grass
(Eragrostis viscosa)

Sticky Love Grass
(Eragrostis viscosa)

Spear Grass
(Heteropogon contortus)

Spear Grass
(Heteropogon contortus)

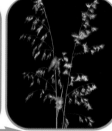

Red Thatching Grass
(Hyparrhenia rufa)

Red Thatching Grass
(Hyparrhenia rufa)

Velvet Grass
(Melenis repens)

Velvet Grass
(Melenis repens)

Buffalo Grass
(Panicum maximum)

Buffalo Grass
(Panicum maximum)

Water Panicum
(Panicum repens)

Water Panicum
(Panicum repens)

Cat's Tail Grass
(Perotis patens)

Cat's Tail Grass
(Perotis patens)

Common Reed
(Phragmites mauritianus)

Common Reed
(Phragmites mauritianus)

VEGETATION – GRASSES

Photographic grass check list continued

Herring-bone Grass
(Pogonarthria squarrosa) ⟷ **Herring-bone Grass**
(Pogonarthria squarrosa)

Sour Grass
(Schmidtia bulbosa) ⟷ **Sour Grass**
(Schmidtia bulbosa)

Golden Bristle Grass
(Setaria sphacelata) ⟷ **Golden Bristle Grass**
(Setaria sphacelata)

Bur-bristle Grass
(Setaria verticillata) ⟷ **Bur-bristle Grass**
(Setaria verticillata)

Wild Sorghum Grass
(Sorghum versicolor) ⟷ **Wild Sorghum Grass**
(Sorghum versicolor)

Confetti Dropseed Grass
(Sporobolus festivus) ⟷ **Confetti Dropseed Grass**
(Sporobolus festivus)

Bushveld Dropseed Grass
(Sporobolus fimbriatus) ⟷ **Bushveld Dropseed Grass**
(Sporobolus fimbriatus)

Pan Dropseed
(Sporobolus iocladus) ⟷ **Pan Dropseed**
(Sporobolus iocladus)

VEGETATION - GRASSES

Spiky Dropseed Grass
(Sporobolus spicatus)

Spiky Dropseed Grass
(Sporobolus spicatus)

Red Oat Grass
(Themeda triandra)

Red Oat Grass
(Themeda triandra)

Spike Carrot-seed Grass
(Tragus berteronianus)

Spike Carrot-seed Grass
(Tragus berteronianus)

Plains' Andropogon
(Andropogon greenwayi)

Plains' Finger Grass
(Digitaria macroblephara)

Pennisetum
(Pennisetum mezianum)

MAMMALS

Wildebeest crossing Lake Ndutu

MAMMALS

Migration

MAMMALS

There is a combination of factors that cause animals to migrate, some of which will be discussed in more detail below. The main reason, however, is to ensure enough food and water throughout the year. In the Serengeti Ecosystem animals basically alternate between the Short Grass Plains in summer and the wooded, tall grass areas in winter. The short grass plains have a low rainfall and lack surface water, except for the temporary pans during the wet season. The tall grass woodland in the north and west have a higher rainfall with perennial rivers.

PALAEONTOLOGICAL EVIDENCE OF THE MIGRATION

The Wildebeest migration in the Serengeti Ecosystem is older than modern man. At Olduvai Gorge there is evidence that the Wildebeest used the Serengeti Plains as seasonal breeding and feeding grounds more than one million years ago, even before our human ancestors learned how to hunt.

WHICH ANIMAL SPECIES MIGRATE?

Wildebeest form the bulk of the migration, being the most numerous. They prefer short grasses but they do eat tall grasses, especially after these have been 'trimmed' by Zebra and Buffalo. They thrive on the new shoots of grasses. *Zebras* form the second largest group of migratory animals and largely follow the same route as the Wildebeest. They congregate on the plains during the rainy season when food is abundant. As soon as food becomes scarce, they break up and disperse in family units. Their dispersal minimises grazing pressure in the low production tall grass areas. *Eland* have the ability to browse (eat leaves) as well as graze (eat grass) and are very well adapted to almost any environment from lowlands to mountains. Although they do not follow the same migratory route as Wildebeest, they also alternate between the plains and the woodland. *Thomson's Gazelles* have a much shorter route than the Wildebeests. They feed only on short grasses, herbs and forbs. They are the first to arrive on the plains and the last to leave. **Grant's Gazelles** do not really need to migrate as they are water-independent but they do move to a limited extent, mainly locally. Their route is in some cases opposite to that of migratory species, spending the rainy season in open patches within the woodland and the dry season on the plains (Estes, 1991).

MIGRATION STATISTICS

How many animals migrate? During good years the Wildebeest population alone may reach up to 1,6 million animals. During the peak of the rainy season the short grass plains support up to two million animals. Census figures during the 1990s estimated the Zebra population at 151 000, the Eland at 12 000, the Thomson's Gazelle at 232 000 and the Grant's Gazelle at 31 000. *How far do they travel?* It is estimated that they travel some 2 000km every year. *How much do they eat?* They consume about 4 000 tons of grass every day, that is about 1,46 million tons of grass per annum. Much of the energy consumed is returned to the soil by means of their droppings.

HISTORY OF ANIMAL COUNTS

The first scientific accounts of animal numbers go back to the 1950s, and were done by Professor Bernhard Grzimek and his son Michael. They divided the Serengeti into counting blocks and counted 99 481 Wildebeests in 1958. At that time the population was at an all-time low because of the Rinderpest epidemic that reached Africa in the early 1900s. It ravaged the continent and killed off millions of wild animals and cattle. The disease persisted in cattle, causing the Wildebeest to become re-infected over and over again for a period of more than 50 years, keeping their numbers low.

The virus was eliminated in cattle only in the 1960s by a strict vaccination campaign. Shortly afterwards, the Wildebeest population started to recover rapidly. Whilst the Wildebeest population was in its diminished stage, the general migratory pattern was from the plains in the east to the rivers in the west and back again. With the rapid recovery of the Wildebeest population, scientists feared massive destruction of the habitat. However, the Wildebeests simply reverted to what was probably their original migratory route before the outbreak of Rinderpest - a circular route starting on the Short Grass Plains, going north to the Masai Mara and back again (see the map on pg102 for details on the route).

The Wildebeest population grew to ±1,3 million and stabilised there in the late 1970s. The limiting factor was probably available grazing. The population reached a peak in 1989, after good rains, when more than 1,6 million Wildebeests were counted. Only once since the recovery did the population go down below the one million mark - that was in 1995 following a severe drought. Today, the population still varies annually between one million and ±1,3 million animals and during very good years it goes up to 1,6 million.

MAMMALS

Wildebeest migration on the plains

MAMMALS

Minerals Research found that the Short Grass Plains contain high levels of phosphate. In contrast, the woodlands showed strong signs of phosphorous deficiency. Phosphorous is very important for growth and lactation, making the plains the ideal place for the migratory animals to have their young. It was found that calcium is available in sufficient quantities in both vegetation types. ***Optimal grass yield*** Grasses are kept in the immature, high nutrient growth stages by continuous, mild grazing. It is easier for herbivores to keep grasses in their optimal stage on the Short Grass Plains, which are low productivity areas, as opposed to the tall grass areas which are high productivity areas. Grasses in high productivity areas become woody at maturity and are then ignored by grazers. ***Relative safety from predators*** Animals can detect predators more easily on the Short Grass Plains, especially during the vulnerable period when they have their young. There is a birth peak in January/February, shortly after arrival on the plains. ***Quick germination of grasses*** The grasses growing on the Short Grass Plains respond immediately to rains, offering almost instant grazing. The reason for this is the solidified layers in the soil, known as 'hard pan' that have the ability to hold water close to the surface, ensuring immediate germination.

Wildebeest migration on the Short Grass Plains

To obtain surface water The main reason for leaving the plains is to get water from the perennial rivers. There is no surface water on the Short Grass Plains, which forces the animals to leave after the rainy season when seasonal pans and puddles dry up. ***To obtain food*** Tall grasslands are high productivity areas and although the grasses are generally lower in nutrients and become woody at maturity, the high biomass (quantity of grass) compensates for it.

WHY DO THEY MOVE OUT OF THE WOODY AREAS?

Waterlogged soils Wildebeests need to move out of waterlogged areas since they are known to develop a foot disease in such soils. Zebra hooves are also not suitable for negotiating soggy areas as they do not have split hooves like antelopes. This causes them to start moving before the onset of the rains. *Tsetse Flies* During the rains the Tsetse Fly becomes more numerous and active. It occurs only in wooded areas as it requires the shade of the trees to rest in during the heat of the day. There are no Tsetse Flies on the Short Grass Areas. *To escape predation* Predators can hide more effectively in tall grass, woody areas which makes it unsuitable for the herbivores (plant-eating animals) to bear and raise their vulnerable young. *Decline in nutrient quality of grass* The nutrient quality of grasses declines in high grass biomass areas, in other words, as soon as the grasses mature, they become woody and unpalatable, losing nutritional value. This means that the grazers will have to take in more food to get the same amount of nutrients and energy.

WHAT IS 'SUCCESSIONAL FEEDING' OR 'FACILITATION'?

'Successional feeding' or 'facilitation' describes a process whereby smaller herbivores benefit from the presence of larger herbivores. Buffaloes do not migrate as such, but they move within huge home ranges. The migratory routes often cross buffalo home ranges and most smaller herbivores benefit from their presence as they feed on the leaves of tall grasses, stimulating them to develop new shoots. In the same way that mowing the lawn stimulates new grass growth, grass is stimulated by grazing and new shoots develop. The Buffaloes also open up areas by trampling, at the same time fertilising the soil with their droppings. After the leaves have been stripped, the zebras move in and further reduce the grasses by nipping off the tough stems with their double set of incisors. This causes the grass to develop fresh, new growth - exactly what the Wildebeests favour. The Thomson's Gazelles, with their small muzzles, cannot utilise tall grasses and they are usually the last to move into the tall grass areas. Although successional feeding seems like a very neat model in theory, it is not always so simplified and animals are by no means dependent on each other to meet their nutritional requirements - it simply makes it easier for them, or 'facilitates' their feeding.

Zebra often move onto the plains before Wildebeest

MAMMALS

M A M M A L S

THE ANNUAL MIGRATION PATTERN IN THE SERENGETI ECOSYSTEM

Currently the migratory herds follows the following general pattern with minor, sometimes major, deviations:

Early dry season (July to October)

This is when the bulk of the migratory herd finds itself in the western corridor, where it crosses the Grumeti River in about June/July/August. Some reach the Mara river already in early August. During September and October some of them spill into the Masai Mara Game Reserve. Some of the herd never go as far north as the Masai Mara Game Reserve.

Late dry season to early wet season (October to December)

In the late dry season bulk of the migratory herd starts its trek south through the Lobo area and along the eastern boundary. Some move straight south through Seronera. Most of the herd will have reached the Short Grass Plains by the middle of January. They have their young in January/February, after which they move around on the plains, following local rainstorms.

Late wet season (April to June)

During this time there is a general movement to the northwest of the plains along the Simiyu, Mbalageti, Seronera and Nyabogati Rivers to the western corridor which they reach in about June. Part of the population moves directly north through Seronera and a smaller section moves north on the eastern side of the Serengeti, through the Loliondo area.

Early wet season (December to April)

During this time the animals are mainly on the Short Grass Plains west of the Gol Mountains in the Ngorongoro Conservation Area, at Gol Kopjes, Barafu Kopjes, Naabi Gate and Lake Ndutu. If there is a dry spell in between, they move west into the Maswa Game Reserve and to the Mbalageti Valley. At the first signs of rain, they move back onto the Serengeti Plains because of the instant availability of new growth.

Large mammals

ENDANGERED SPECIES

The following animals occur on the 1994 IUCN Red List of Threatened Animals:
* African Hunting Dog (endangered)
* African Elephant (endangered)
* Black Rhinoceros (endangered)
* Cheetah (vulnerable)

The following animals were identified as threatened with extinction on the CITES list:
* Black Rhinoceros
* African Elephant
* Leopard
* Cheetah
* Pangolin

NUMBER OF SPECIES IN THE SERENGETI NATIONAL PARK

Some 135 species of mammals have been recorded in the Serengeti, of which 20 are bats and 26 are mice, rats and gerbils. Very little work has been done on the bats and small rodents, so chances are that there are many more unrecorded species in these two groups. There are 22 antelope species of which the Blue Duiker, Greater Kudu, Lesser Kudu, Mountain Reedbuck and Oryx are the rarest and are seldom seen.

INTERESTING FACTS ABOUT LARGE MAMMALS

Take note: The estimated population numbers provided below are largely based on figures provided in the Serengeti National Park Management Plan 1991-1995. This excludes the Masai Mara Game Reserve in Kenya.

Elephant

Elephants can be found mainly in the heavily wooded Seronera and Lobo areas where both breeding herds and lone bulls can be found. The Elephant population inside the Serengeti is gradually growing because of increased commercial agriculture and cattle farming on the outside. The breeding herds are led by a dominant female - a social system referred to as 'matriarchal'. The herds vary from ±10 to 60 and a bull will only join the herd when a female is in estrous - when she is ready to mate or is ovulating. Bulls form small groups of 4 to 10 and older males are often solitary. The elephant population for the Serengeti was estimated at ±400 to 500 during a census in 1986. It escalated to ±980 in 1992, to 1 357 in 1994 and is now believed to be more than 2 000. An Elephant eats about 280kg to 300kg of food per day which takes ±24 hours to digest.

On average they produce droppings every hour, fertilizing the soil in the process. The fertilizing process is enhanced by the activity of dung beetles, which roll the dung into balls, lay their eggs in it an then bury the balls. Elephants replace their teeth six times in their life time. New teeth are formed in the back of the mouth and the old teeth in the front of the mouth break off. Their roots are assimilated into the bone, almost in conveyor-belt fashion. Elephants chew by rolling their molars backwards and forwards, not sideways like other herbivores. When their last set of teeth become worn down, it becomes difficult for them to eat and in severe cases they die of starvation.

Hippopotamus

Hippos occur in fresh-water rivers and pools. Most of their day is spent in the water and at night they get out to feed, almost exclusively on grasses. Because of their low energy expenditure and slow metabolism, their food intake is much lower (about 50%) relative to that of other herbivores. They eat about 130kg of food in one night, which takes an average of two days and two nights to digest. They do not ruminate.

A hippo cannot sweat, but when it lies in the sun, the skin secretes a reddish liquid which minimises water loss and protects the skin against sunburn. That is why hippos 'turn pink' in the sun. They can stay under water for about five minutes and even give birth under water. In the Serengeti hippos occur mainly in the perennial rivers such as the Grumeti, the Mara, the Mbalageti and in pools in the Seronera river.

Rhinoceros

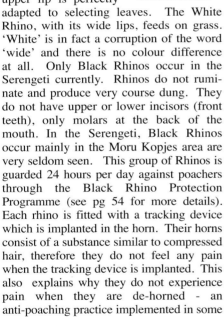

Black Rhinos are browsers (leaf-eaters) and their pointed upper lip is perfectly adapted to selecting leaves. The White Rhino, with its wide lips, feeds on grass. 'White' is in fact a corruption of the word 'wide' and there is no colour difference at all. Only Black Rhinos occur in the Serengeti currently. Rhinos do not ruminate and produce very course dung. They do not have upper or lower incisors (front teeth), only molars at the back of the mouth. In the Serengeti, Black Rhinos occur mainly in the Moru Kopjes area are very seldom seen. This group of Rhinos is guarded 24 hours per day against poachers through the Black Rhino Protection Programme (see pg 54 for more details). Each rhino is fitted with a tracking device which is implanted in the horn. Their horns consist of a substance similar to compressed hair, therefore they do not feel any pain when the tracking device is implanted. This also explains why they do not experience pain when they are de-horned - an anti-poaching practice implemented in some areas in southern Africa.

Buffalo

Buffaloes are common in the Serengeti and occur throughout the park in wooded, tall grass areas with plenty of water. They are almost exclusively grazers, preferring the leaves of tall grasses. They roam in very large territories and form herds of up to 2 000. Within the herds are cows, calves and a number of breeding and non-breeding males. Small bachelor groups or lone bulls often separate from the herd. The large herds play a vital part in opening up tall grass areas for other grazers by means of trampling, grazing and fertilizing the soil. During the heat of the day they often seek out shade in which to rest and ruminate. Buffalo numbers in the Serengeti Ecosystem are estimated at ±67 000.

Giraffe

Giraffe are plentiful in the Serengeti and occur in woodland, especially *Acacia* woodland - their favourite food source. They only browse, using their long tongues to select fresh leaves and pods. They can be seen stripping thorny *Acacia* branches with their lips, seemingly oblivious of the thorns. Their thick, rubbery lips have evolved to cope with the sharp thorns. Giraffes form very loose associations, the bond between mother and her young being the strongest. Like other vertebrates, they have seven neck vertebrae, each one being ±40cm long. They have specially adapted valves in the neck arteries and veins to control their blood pressure when they lower their heads to drink. If the blood was allowed to rush freely to the brain, they would pass out every time they lowered their heads to drink water. The Giraffe species found in the Serengeti is commonly known as the 'Maasai Giraffe' and can be distinguished by the irregular, star-shaped markings on their skins. The estimated number of Giraffes in the Serengeti ecosystem is about 12 500.

Zebra

Zebras are very successful as a herbivore species. Surprisingly, their population was not affected by the Rinderpest outbreak early in the 19th century and it has been fairly stable since.

MAMMALS

It remains a mystery to science how they have managed to maintain their numbers with increased competition from the expanding Wildebeest population, predation and poaching. Their strong social system and their adaptability partially account for their success as a species. They are equally well adapted to feed on tall and short grasses, having both top and bottom incisors. This enables them to nip off tough grass stems and to feed on fresh, green grasses. As soon as food becomes scarce, they break up and disperse in family units. Their dispersal minimises grazing pressure in low production areas. Even though they disperse, they are still fairly safe from predators because of the fierce protective instincts of the dominant stallion. Zebras do not ruminate and therefore the food passes faster through their digestive system and their droppings are coarser. Their population in the Serengeti Ecosystem is estimated at ±260 000.

The White-bearded Wildebeest

The Wildebeest is a migratory species (read more about the migration on pg 98). Rutting takes place from May to June whilst they are on the move. It is limited to a very short period so that births can be synchronised to provide more protection against predators. The bulls establish very small, temporary territories which they defend vehemently. The females circulate within these territories and a male actively tries to claim them as soon as they move into his territory, by means of herding. This is usually accompanied by a show of hoof-stamping, head-shaking, snorts and a whole lot of attitude and stance. Their antics have earned them the title of 'clowns of the bush'. However, severe head-shaking and galloping around in circles is sometimes not funny at all. It can be the result of bot-fly larvae infestations in the mucous membranes of the nasal passages. The eggs of the bot-fly hatch inside the body of the female fly and are deposited in the nostrils of the Wildebeest. The larvae crawl up the nostrils, attach themselves to the mucous membranes and grow to maturity (± nine month period). At maturity they may be as large as 2,5 x 1cm.

They then usually get sneezed out, where they pupate in the ground. However, the larvae can cause infections by crawling into the eye sockets or into the brain.

Eland

Eland have the ability to browse as well as graze and are very well adapted to almost any environment from lowlands to mountains. Their number in the Serengeti Ecosystem is estimated at about 13 800. They do migrate but do not necessarily follow the same route as the Wildebeest.

Topi

The highest population of Topi anywhere in Africa can be found along the Mbalageti River and in the Handajega area. There are also resident groups in the Seronera Valley. The Topi is strictly a grazer and often occupies transitional zones between grassland and woodland typical of the Seronera area within the Serengeti. Its narrow muzzle is adapted to select the most tender green leaf blades. Topi do not have to drink when their fodder is green. Their population is estimated to be ±78 000.

Roan Antelope

The Mbalageti valley is also one of the few havens for Roan Antelope. Roan is one of the rarest antelopes in the Serengeti. They feed selectively on taller grasses that grow on leached, poor soils. This kind of grassland supports a low herbivore biomass and offers little nourishment in the dry season. For this reason Roan Antelope territories are very large. Low production areas have the advantage of eliminating competition but nevertheless, Roan Antelopes often appear under-fed during the late dry season. They are highly territorial and herds of 5 to 20 are often, but not always, accompanied by a dominant male.

MAMMALS

Coke's Hartebeest

Kongoni or Coke's Hartebeest occur in small herds of 5 to 15 animals and can be seen in most parts of the park. There is a surprisingly large population of Kongoni in the Serengeti Ecosystem, numbering almost 23 000. They prefer medium grassland and are often associated with Red Oat Grass (*Themeda triandra*). Males establish territories and female herds circulate within these territories.

Defassa Waterbuck

The Defassa Waterbuck is entirely dependent on water and therefore only occurs in close proximity to permanent, fresh water. It feeds on medium to short grasses in marshy areas and often ventures into the water to feed. The Waterbuck has glands that are spread over most of the body, known as 'diffuse glands'. The main purpose of the glands is to make the skin impermeable to water but, the secretion renders the meat slightly unpleasant to predators and to humans. Interestingly, the meat only takes on that taste if it comes into direct contact with the outside of the skin. A group of females and young are mostly accompanied by a dominant male but satellite males often occur on the periphery of the herd. A Waterbuck has no physiological adaptations to survive under severe heat stress. The only way it copes with high temperatures, is to pant and to sweat, lowering its temperature by evaporative cooling. This can triple its waterloss and it may loose up to 30 litres of water under extreme heat conditions. To counter the loss, it will need to drink at least 60 litres of water. Compare that with the Oryx which has specialised physiological adaptations which causes it to loose only 4 litres of water under the same circumstances. An Oryx can survive without drinking surface water.

Bohor Reedbuck

The Bohor Reedbuck is extremely shy but it can be seen near swampy areas, floodplains and along rivers. They live in loose, monogamous pairs but lack the social interaction such as grooming and do not mark their territories. During droughts or after veld fires, a larger number of Bohor Reedbuck will congregate in suitable areas. The Reedbuck is mainly a grazer, having the ability to subsist on course grasses that are unpalatable and in many cases inaccessible to other antelope species. The tall grass areas that they favour, are also an essential requirement for concealment.

Bushbuck

Bushbuck occur in heavily wooded areas along rivers and are not commonly seen in the Serengeti. Their cryptic colorations makes for excellent camouflage. They are very sensitive to disturbance such as overgrazing by other herbivores and cattle and will soon move to undisturbed areas. If there is none left, their numbers diminish rapidly. They are solitary, the main bond being between mother and offspring. Bushbuck are not territorial and home ranges often overlap. They are predominantly browsers, but will feed on tender, green grasses as well.

Grant's Gazelle

Grant's Gazelle can be seen everywhere in the Serengeti National Park but are more numerous on the Short Grass Plains. They can often be seen in association with the smaller Thomson's Gazelle, but Grant's Gazelles have the advantage of being able to tolerate drier habitats and can survive without any surface water.

They can therefore remain on the plains during the dry season. Even though they are intermediate feeders, they browse (eat leaves) more than graze (eat grass) and are more likely to occur in closed habitats than the Thomson's Gazelle. They are migratory but, interestingly, they often move in the reverse direction of the other migratory species. A portion of the population prefers smaller plains within woodland zones during the rainy season and the Short Grass Plains during the dry season. The rest of the population utilises the plains in the rainy season and withdraw to the edge of the woodland during the dry season (Estes, 1991). They are not nearly as numerous as the Thomson's Gazelle as their estimated number is only ±31 000.

Thomson's Gazelle

The Thomson's Gazelle is an intermediate feeder, grazing on green, short grasses and browsing on herbs, forbs, shrubs and legumes during the dry season. They do migrate, but their migratory circuit is shorter than that of the Wildebeest. They capitalise on tall grass areas that have been reduced by larger grazers. Although they are water-dependent, at least some males do remain on the water-less plains during the dry season. They have the ability to feed on very short grasses and are always the first to arrive and the last to leave the plains. During the dry season they occupy the edge of the woodland and islands within the woodland zone (Estes, 1991). They are one of the most numerous antelopes in the Serengeti Ecosystem with an estimated population of ±440 000.

Impala

Impala is an ecotone species, preferring areas on the edge of woodland and grass-land, much like the Topi. The Impala prefers light woodland and its small hoof size restricts it to well-drained areas that provide firm footing.

They are water dependent but when their food is green, they do not need to drink. Their territories are always in close vicinity to permanent water. The Impala is an inter-mediate feeder, suggesting that it eats leaves and grass. They thrive in over-utilised areas and are very adaptable in their food require-ments, readily eating grass, leaves, fallen leaves and fruits. Their split upper lip enables them to feed on very shortgrasses close to the ground such as grass sprouts or grass that has already been cropped by other grazers. In the Serengeti they prefer *Acacia/Commiphora* woodland on or near ecotones, utilising the upper slopes in the rainy season and moving down to drainage line greenbelts in the dry season (Estes, 1991). Seronera is a typical example of an ecotone. Impalas are highly territorial dur-ing the rut (May-June) when dominant males establish relatively small territories and noisily herd the females into their domains. A successful male with the most desirable territory, may round up 50 to 100 females. Young and non-breeding males form bachelor herds but after the rut they freely intermingle with breeding herds. The Impala population for the Serengeti Ecosystem is estimated at ±109 000.

Oribi

Oribi occur in tall grass areas and they are most common in the north-western corner of the Serengeti. They avoid woodland and bush but prefer grassland that is not too tall or dense, such as floodplains and montane grassland. The Oribi is the only dwarf antelope that feeds almost exclusively on grass. They are often associ-ated with larger herbivores such as Buffalo and Zebra, benefitting from the reduction of the habitat through trampling and grazing. Their social organisation varies between monogamous pairs and polygynous groups. Males have territories which they share with one or up to five females but some of the females may be offspring. They are usually the first to move into recently burnt areas.

Steinbok

The Steinbok is a dwarf antelope that occurs in dry areas and can often be seen next to the road. They benefit from over-utilised and destructed areas, thriving on recovering vegetation. They are not water-dependent. Since they feed on grass as well as shrubs and herbs, they are called 'intermediate feeders'. They feed very selectively, seeking out only the tastiest bits. They have an interesting habit of covering up their droppings to disguise their presence to predators. Pairs seem to share the same territory but they seldom spend time together.

Common Duiker

The Common Duiker is a very adaptable species, using a variety of habitats and food plants. The only criteria is sufficient cover. They are mainly browsers, feeding on fruits and foliage of small shrubs and herbs. Surprisingly, they even ingest caterpillars, lizards, rodents and birds. Duikers do not mate for life but are mainly solitary, with males and females living in adjacent home ranges, associating only during courtship.

Kirk's Dik-dik

The Kirk's Dik-dik prefers areas that are sparsely covered in grass and shrubs, especially stony ground. In the Serengeti they are often associated with *Aloe* and *Sansevieria* vegetation communities. They are common along the Banagi Loop which is quite rocky. The Dik-dik is well adapted to survive under heat stress, their extended snout enlarging the mucosa area used for evaporative cooling. The larger nose cavity increases the airflow but the tiny nostrils prevent water loss to the outside (Estes, 1991). They occur in pairs or can be solitary. Dik-diks have the fastest metabolism of all antelope, needing to feed every hour day and night. They select only the tastiest bits of plants, including fruits - this makes them 'concentrate selectors'. Their small muzzle is ideal for selecting the sweetest bits of food. They occasionally stand on their hind legs to reach higher whilst feeding. They form closely associated monogamous pairs and are territorial. Their limbs are more flexible than most other ungulates, being able to stretch their legs straight forward when lying down - a position observed only in goats and Did-diks.

Klipspringer

The Klipspringer's coat is very thick, the hairs hollow, brittle and loose - an anti-predator adaptation in that a predator can easily loose its grip on the loose hairs. The thick coat and hollow hairs have the function of insulating the animal against extreme heat and cold - climatic conditions that are often associated with hills. They feed on evergreen shrubs such as *Sansevieria*, *Aloe* sp., *Euphorbia* sp. as well as fruits, berries and seed pods. They will also leave their kopje habitat to feed on freshly sprouted grasses. They do not need to drink, obtaining enough moisture from their food. Klipspringers are territorial and form closely associated monogamous pairs.

Lion

The Serengeti probably has the largest Lion population in Africa. Males are in their prime at five or six years of age when they have the ability to take over a pride from an older male. Two brothers often remain together, making it easier to oust another dominant male. When they take over a pride they kill the young cubs and even some of the older ones. It is touching to see how the females try to defend their cubs or try to lead them away, but they stand defenceless against the males.

M A M M A L S

After the cubs have been killed the female almost immediately comes into estrous, in other words she becomes ready to mate. Although this seems cruel, it is nature's way of ensuring that the genes of the strongest Lion, and not that of its predecessor, will continue the line. The males rarely hold on to a pride for longer than three years, usually shorter. Lions are very sociable animals and they love to play. The females of a pride are often related and it is not unusual for females of the same pride to suckle each other's cubs. Some Lions remain in their territories throughout the year but others, especially young adult Lions, become nomadic and follow the migration. This is risky, especially for males, because by doing so they move through other established territories and risk being killed. The Lion population in the Serengeti Ecosystem is estimated at about 2 800 individuals.

Cheetah

The Cheetah is the fastest land mammal, being able to sprint at ±120kph, but they can only maintain that speed for about 100m. They are diurnal. Cheetahs differ from other cats in that they are not able to retract their claws. They are thus not able to climb trees vertically but the claws do give them extra grip when they sprint. Their spinal cord is extremely flexible and stretch more than that of any other sprinting animal, adding to their speed. Theoretically, it can be calculated that a Cheetah would be able to run 'catterpillar-style' at 10km an hour, based only on the spine's ability to stretch and retract. Their population is estimated at about 300 on the plains and about 600 within the ecosystem.

Leopard

Leopards are plentiful in the Serengeti but because of their secretive lifestyle and their nocturnal habits, they are not commonly seen. Leopards favour heavily wooded areas, hills, kopjes and riverine forest and are thus more common in the Seronera and Lobo areas. They spend much of their time in trees and have the ability to take a middle-sized antelope up into a tree with little effort. They do this to secure their prey from other predators and scavengers. If the intestines of the prey fall to the ground the Leopard will painstakingly cover them with soil to conceal the smell. Leopards are solitary and adult males and females only associate during mating.

Hyena

The Serengeti ecosystem has the largest Hyena population in all of Africa. One can see packs of more than 40 animals. The Hyena is also the most abundant predator in the Serengeti, estimated at 7 500. Their dens consist of several burrows in close proximity to each other. Much of the day is spent sleeping but they are active at night. They not only scavenge but also hunt, putting them right at the top of the food chain with the Lion. A dominant female is the leader of the pack, making it a matriarchal society. Females are larger than males and the genitals of both sexes look alike, females having a pseudo-penis. A hyena has the strongest jaws of all animals, being able to crush the bones to manageable pieces that they can swallow. They are able to digest bones very effectively and therefore produce calcium-rich droppings that turn white when dry. They share an ancestry with Civets, both having an unusual digestive physiology which can break down complicated organic compounds. In this manner, Hyenas can 'detoxify' the rotten meat that they so often feed on whilst scavenging.

MAMMALS

African Hunting Dog

The African Hunting Dog or Cape Hunting Dog is one of the rarest predators in the Serengeti although they were fairly common on the plains during the sixties. They occur on the 1994 IUCN Red List of threatened animals as well as on the CITES list of animals threatened with extinction. Hunting Dogs were shot on site, as vermin, in wildlife parks all over Africa from the early 1900s to as late as the 1960s. In the late 1960s some 153 Hunting Dogs roamed the Serengeti Plains. In 1970, 12 packs with 95 adults were counted and in 1978 a dramatic drop was recorded - only seven packs with 26 adults. In the early 1980s only one pack remained on the plains (Estes, 1991). Today, Hunting Dogs are not seen at all on the plains. There may possibly be some left along the Mbalageti River.

Why the sharp decline? It is a combination of factors. Firstly, they have a unique social system and their successful survival depends on large packs. Hunting Dog packs have only one alpha male and one alpha female that breed. The rest of the pack are helpers. Unlike most sociable mammals, Hunting Dog male offspring remain in the natal pack and the females emigrate. When the pack goes hunting, at least one member of the pack remains at the den to look after the pups. All members partake in the raising of the pups. After a hunt each member will regurgitate a portion of its food to the young ones. This feeding frenzy is accompanied by excited squeals and darting around. It can be a messy business but Hooded Vultures usually hang around the den for easy pickings, cleaning up in the process. It was found that the Hunting Dog pack sizes declined dramatically since the 1960s, especially the pup survival rate.

A low pup survival rate means there are less pups in the pack and less food available. Another reason for their decline may be the unusually large populations of Lions and Hyenas in the Serengeti. Both species kill them without provocation. Thirdly, Hunting Dogs are extremely vulnerable to various canine diseases carried by domestic dogs, Distemper being one of the deadliest. In this way entire packs have been wiped out and alarmingly, some of the diseases that they succumb to, have not yet been diagnosed.

Aardwolf

The Aardwolf resembles a Hyena but it is unique in that it feeds almost exclusively on Harvester Termites. Its distribution therefore closely corresponds with the distribution of Harvester Termites (*Trinervitermes* and *Hodotermes*). These termites favour over-grazed, sandy areas. The nocturnal *Trinervitermes* constitutes the Aardwolf's summer diet and the diurnal *Hodotermes* forms the winter diet. The Aardwolf locates the Harvester Termites by listening for them with its large ears held close to the ground. They lap the termites up with their broad tongue which is accommodated in a particularly broad palate. Although their canine teeth are well developed, the molars (back teeth) are reduced to mere pegs. Their digestive system is adapted to digest the terpene chemicals present in the termites. They ingest lots of sand whilst feeding and their droppings consist of a high percentage of sand, making them unusually heavy. They make use of communal toilets. The skin around the muzzle is hairless, leathery and tough to resist the terpene chemicals squirted by the soldier termites in defence. Because of the high fat content of their diet they do not need to feed very often.

Bat-eared Fox

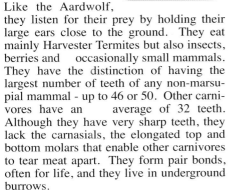

Another dog-like animal that feeds almost exclusively on termites, is the Bat-eared Fox. Like the Aardwolf, they listen for their prey by holding their large ears close to the ground. They eat mainly Harvester Termites but also insects, berries and occasionally small mammals. They have the distinction of having the largest number of teeth of any non-marsupial mammal - up to 46 or 50. Other carnivores have an average of 32 teeth. Although they have very sharp teeth, they lack the carnasials, the elongated top and bottom molars that enable other carnivores to tear meat apart. They form pair bonds, often for life, and they live in underground burrows.

Warthog

The Warthog is the only wild pig that mainly grazes, which it does during the rainy season when grasses are green. During the dry season they concentrate on uprooting rhizomes, bulbs and tubers - a function they are well equipped for by the presence of tusks and a disc-shaped snout. The tusks are elongated canines, the lower of which is razor-sharp. They have 'warts' or out-growths on their faces to cushion the blows and to protect them during fighting. The males have two pairs and the females only one. Warthogs do not ruminate. They often graze and root by standing on their calloused 'knees'. They have a matriarchal social system but share home ranges with bachelor and solitary males, preferring savannah woodland. Since they have managed to secure a food source high in protein which is largely ignored by other animals - roots and bulbs - they can afford to spend more time sleeping. They are therefore diurnal and spend the night in burrows. During the day they like to wallow in mud to rid them of insects and to cool them down. Warthogs are non-territorial. Their population is estimated at ±5 600.

Bushpig

Bushpigs are far less common than warthogs and they are more secretive, being mainly nocturnal. They are very adaptable in habitat choice, occurring in montane forest, marshes, swamps, woodland - as long as there is sufficient food and concealment. They feed mainly on roots, fruits and bulbs, but they also eat carrion, bones, excrement and small mammals. Unlike the warthog, they live in one-male harems or family groups. They are non-territorial. Bushpigs do not burrow, but rest in dense thickets during the day and feed only at night.

MAMMALS

Baby Hyenas

'Hear no evil, see no evil, do no evil'

Mammal check list

Take note: *Where there is a significant difference in the male and female animal, a photograph of the head of the opposite sex will be provided (where available). Otherwise, differences will be pointed out.*

Abbreviations: Sw: Swahili; **Ger:** German; **Fr:** French. **Height:** Shoulder height. **Length:** From nose to rump excluding tail. **Sex diff:** Sexual difference. **Soc. Org:** Social organisation.

ANIMALS – MAMMALS

Mega-herbivores

E: African Elephant   Sw: Tembo

African Elephant *(Loxodonto africana)*
Sw: Tembo   **Ger:** Grosselephant   **Fr:** L´ Elephant d' Afrique

Height: M 350cm; F 300cm
Weight: M 5 750kg; F 3 800kg
Gestation: 22 months
Litter: One
Life span: 65 years
Active: Day and night

Sex diff: Males larger with rounded head and larger tusks
Habitat: Savannah, scrub
Food: Leaves, bark, fruit, grass
Soc. Org: Gregarious, herds of 10-50. Matriarchal, non-territorial

E: Black Rhinoceros   Sw: Faru

Black Rhinoceros *(Diceros bicornis)*
Sw: Faru   **Ger:** Spitzmaulnashorn   **Fr:** Le `Rhinocéros noir

Height: 135 - 230cm
Weight: 700 - 1 600kg
Gestation: 15 months
Litter: One
Life span: 40 years
Active: Day and night

Sex diff: Cows slightly larger
Habitat: Woodland
Food: Trees, shrubs, leaves and forbs (small herbs)
Soc. Org: Solitary or cow & calf/calves, territorial

E: Hippopotamus   Sw: Kiboko

Hippopotamus *(Hippopotamus amphibius)*
Sw: Kiboko   **Ger:** Grossflusspferd   **Fr:** L'Hippopotame amphibié

Height: M 150 cm; F 144 cm
Weight: M ± 2 300kg, F ± 1 900
Gestation: 8 months
Litter: One
Life span: ± 40 years
Active: Day and night

Sex diff: Males larger
Habitat: Aquatic, grassland
Food: Grass
Soc. Org: Gregarious with one dominent male, territorial

Buffalo, Zebra and Giraffe

E: Buffalo Sw: Mbogo

Buffalo *(Syncerus caffer)*
Sw: Mbogo/Nyati   **Ger:** Kaffernbüffel   **Fr:** Le Buffle d `Afrique

Height: 140 - 170cm
Weight: M 785kg; F 715kg
Gestation: 11 months
Litter: One
Life span: ± 23 years
Active: Day and night

Sex diff: Horns of male have thicker boss
Habitat: Woodland, tall grass areas
Food: Tall grasses, leaves & shoots
Soc. Org: Gregarious, territorial in large home ranges

Mammal check list

Zebra *(Equus quagga boehmi)*
Sw: Punda milia **Ger:** Steppenzebra **Fr:** Le Zébre de steppe

Height: ± 134cm

Weight: M ± 290kg; F ± 210kg

Gestation: 12 months

Litter: One

Life span: 35 years

Active: Day and night

Sex diff: Males more stout

Habitat: Grass and savannah woodland

Food: Tall and short grasses

Soc. Org: Harems with one male and ± 3-6 females, non-territorial

E: Zebra   Sw: Punda milia

Giraffe *(Giraffa camelopardalis)*
Sw: Twiga **Ger:** Giraffe **Fr:** La Giraffe

Height: ± 3m to the shoulder; 4.5 - 5m total

Weight: M ± 1 850kg; F ± 825kg

Gestation: 15 months

Litter: One

Life span: 28 years

Active: Day and night

Food: *Acacia* leaves, pods

Sex diff: Males more heavily built, horns thicker

Habitat: *Acacia* savannah woodland

Soc. Org: Loose herd structure, groups of ± 4 - 20, non-territorial

E: Giraffe   Sw: Twiga

The Cat family

Lion *(Panthera leo)*
Sw: Simba **Ger:** Löwe **Fr:** Le Lion

Height: M 115cm; F 91cm

Weight: M ± 220kg; F ± 150kg

Gestation: 3,5 months

Litter: 1 - 4

Life span: 20 years

Active: Mostly nocturnal

Sex. diff: Males larger with mane

Habitat: Varied - forest to desert

Food: Meat, mainly ungulates

Soc. Org: Prides of 2 - 30 animals with one dominant male or two brothers, territorial

E: Lion (male)   Sw: Simba

Leopard *(Panthera pardus)*
Sw: Chui **Ger:** Leopard **Fr:** La Panthère d'Afrique

Height: 65cm

Weight: M ± 60kg; F ± 40kg

Gestation: 3 months

Litter: 2 - 3

Life span: 20 years

Active: Nocturnal

Sex diff: Males larger

Habitat: Woodland, riverine forest, mountains, kopjes

Food: Meat, middle-sized ungulates and small mammals

Soc. Org: Solitary, territorial

E: Leopard   Sw: Chui

ANIMALS – MAMMALS

ANIMALS – MAMMALS

E: Cheetah   Sw: Msongo/Duma

Cheetah *(Acinonyx jubatus)*
Sw: Msongo/Duma   **Ger:** Gepard   **Fr:** Le Guépard

Height: 86cm
Weight: M ± 50kg; F ± 42kg
Gestation: 3 months
Litter: 1 - 5
Life span: 16 years
Active: Diurnal

Sex diff: Males slightly heavier
Habitat: Open woodland & grassland plains
Food: Meat, smaller ungulates and other small animals and birds
Soc. Org: Pairs, mothers with cubs, solitary, non-territorial

E: Serval   Sw: Mondo

Serval *(Felis serval)*
Sw: Mondo   **Ger:** Servalkatze   **Fr:** Le Serval

Height: 56cm
Weight: M 14kg; F 9kg
Gestation: 2 months
Litter: 1 - 4
Life span: 13-20 years
Active: Mainly noncturnal

Sex diff: Males slightly heavier
Habitat: Moist bushland, riverine forest
Food: Small mammals and birds
Soc. Org: Solitary or mother with young

E: Caracal   Sw: Simba mangu

Caracal *(Felis caracal)*
Sw: Simba mangu   **Ger:** Wüstenluchs   **Fr:** Le Caracal

Height: 43cm
Weight: M ± 15kg; F ± 10kg
Gestation: 2 months
Litter: 2 - 4
Life span: 11 years
Active: Mainly nocturnal

Sex diff: Males slightly heavier
Habitat: Dry *Acacia* bushland, semi-desert and rocky areas
Food: Small mammals and birds
Soc. Org: Solitary or mother with young

E: African Wild Cat   Sw: Paka mwiti

African Wild Cat *(Felis silvestris lybica)*
Sw: Paka mwiti   **Ger:** Wildkatze   **Fr:** Le Chat gante' d 'Afrique

Height: 25cm
Weight: M 5kg; F 4kg
Gestation: 2 months
Litter: 1 - 5
Life span: Not known
Active: Mainly nocturnal

Sex diff: Males slightly larger
Habitat: Varied, requires tall grass or rocks
Food: Small rodents, birds, insects
Soc. Org: Solitary or mother with young

Mammal check list

The Pig family

Warthog *(Phacochoerus aethiopicus)*
Sw: Ngiri **Ger:** Warzenschwein **Fr:** Le Phacochére

Height: M 70cm; F 60cm
Weight: M ± 100kg; F ± 60kg
Gestation: 5,5 months
Litter: 1 - 8
Life span: 20 years
Active: Diurnal

Sex diff: Males larger with 2 pairs of warts, female 1 pair
Habitat: Open woodland & water
Food: Roots, rhizomes, fruit, grass
Soc. Org: Family groups of 4 - 10, matriarchal, non-territorial

E: Warthog   Sw: Ngiri

Bushpig *(Potamochoerus larvatus)*
Sw: Nguruwe **Ger:** Buschschwein **Fr:** Le Potamochére d`Afrique

Height: 70 - 100cm
Weight: M 120kg; F 70kg
Gestation: 4 months
Litter: 2 - 3
Life span: 20 years
Active: Nocturnal

Sex diff: Males larger
Habitat: Woodland, riverine forest, mountains
Food: Roots, rhizomes, fruit, grass and they scavenge
Soc. Org: Solitary

E: Bushpig   Sw: Nguruwe

The Dog family

Spotted Hyena *(Crocuta crocuta)*
Sw: Fisi/Nyangao **Ger:** Fleckenhyäne **Fr:** Le Hyèna tachetée

Height: 77cm
Weight: M 63kg; F 70kg
Gestation: 4 months
Litter: 1 - 4
Life span: 25 years
Active: Nocturnal

Sex diff: Females larger than males
Habitat: Varied, grassland or woodland and semi-desert
Food: Carrion and also hunt
Soc. Org: Gregarious, dominant female, matriarchal, territorial

E: Spotted Hyena   Sw: Fisi/Nyangao

African Hunting Dog *(Lycaon pictus)*
Sw: Mbwai mwitu **Ger:** Hyänenhund **Fr:** Le Cynhyène

Height: 68cm
Weight: 20 - 36kg
Gestation: 2,5 months
Litter: ± 14
Life span: 12 years
Active: Diurnal

Sex diff: None
Habitat: Open woodland
Food: Meat, mammals
Soc. Org: Gregarious, packs of 6-30, dominant male and female, non-territorial

E: African Hunting Dog Sw: Mbwai mwitu

The Dog family continued

Burger Cillié

E: Aardwolf   Sw: Fisi ya nkole

Aardwolf *(Protelus cristatus)*
Sw: Fisi ya nkole **Ger:** Erdwolf **Fr:** Le Protèle

Height: 50cm

Weight: 11kg

Gestation: 2,5 months

Litter: 2 - 4

Life span: 13 years

Active: Nocturnal

Sex diff: None

Habitat: Open woodland, grassland, semi-desert

Food: Harvester termites

Soc. Org: Usually solitary or mother and young, territorial

E: Golden Jackal   Sw: Bweha wa mbuga

Golden Jackal *(Canis aureus)*
Sw: Bweha wa mbuga **Ger:** Goldschakal **Fr:** Le Chacal commun

Height: 43cm

Weight: 12,5kg

Gestation: 2 months

Litter: 3 - 8

Life span: 10 - 12 years

Active: Day and Night

Sex diff: None

Habitat: Open country with good cover and water

Food: Carrion, small mammals and birds, also sugarcane, maize and green crops - omnivorous

Soc. Org: Pairs for life, territorial, may form group territories

Side-striped Jackal *(Canis adustus)*
Sw: Bweha **Ger:** Streifenschakal **Fr:** Chacal à flancs rayés

Height: 39cm

Weight: M 9,7kg; F 8,7kg

Gestation: 2 - 2,5 months

Litter: 2 - 6

Life span: 11 years

Active: Day and Night

Sex diff: Males slightly larger

Habitat: Thick woodland with plenty water

Food: Carrion, fruit, hares, rodents

Soc. Org: Solitary or pairs for life, also family groups, territorial

---

E: Side-striped Jackal   Sw: Bweha

Black-backed Jackal *(Canis mesomelas)*
Sw: Bweha nyekundu **Ger:** Schabrackenschakal **Fr:** Le Chacal à chabraque

Height: 38cm

Weight: M 10kg; F 8kg

Gestation: 2 months

Litter: 1 - 6

Life span: 13 years

Active: Day and Night

Sex diff: Males slightly larger

Habitat: Very well adapted in all habitats

Food: Carrion, small mammals

Soc. Org: Solitary or pairs for life, also family groups, territorial

E: Black-backed Jackal   Sw: Bweha nyekundu

ANIMALS – MAMMALS

Mammal check list

The Dog family continued

Bat-eared Fox *(Otocyon megalotis)*
Sw: Bweha masigio **Ger:** Löffelhund **Fr:** L'Otocyon

Height: 25 -30cm
Weight: M 3,8kg; F 4,2kg
Gestation: 2 months
Litter: 2 - 6
Life span: 12 years
Active: Day and Night
Sex diff: Females slightly larger

Habitat: Open dry bush or semi-desert
Food: Mostly termites, insects, occasionally small rodents
Soc. Org: Pairs or family of up to 8, territorial

E: Bat-eared Fox Sw: Bweha masigio

The large Antelopes

Eland *(Taurotragus oryx)*
Sw: Pofu **Ger:** Elanantilope **Fr:** L'Eland/'Elan du Cap

Height: M 170cm; F 145cm
Weight: M ± 800kg; ± F 480kg
Gestation: 9 months
Litter: One
Life span: 25 years
Active: Mainly diurnal
Sex diff: Males much larger

Habitat: Varied, from open plains to mountains to semi-deserts
Food: Mainly leaves, fruit, also grass in summer
Soc. Org: Gregarious, small herds of 8-12 or very large herds. Very large home ranges

E: Eland   Sw: Pofu

Roan *(Hippotragus aquinus)*
Sw: Korongo **Ger:** Pferdeantilope **Fr:** L'Hippotrague /Le Rouanne

Height: 143cm
Weight: ± 260kg
Gestation: 9,5 months
Litter: One
Life span: ± 17 years
Active: Mainly diurnal
Sex diff: Males slightly larger

Habitat: Open woodland near water, tall grass areas
Food: Tall grasses
Soc. Org: Gregarious, herds of 5 - 25 with dominant male and female, territorial within large home ranges

E: Roan   Sw: Korongo

Defassa Waterbuck *(Kobus ellipsiprymnus)*
Sw: Kuru **Ger:** Wasserbuck **Fr:** Le Cobe Defassa

Height: M 135cm; F 120cm
Weight: M ± 250kg; F ± 175kg
Gestation: 8,5 months
Litter: One
Life span: ± 18 years
Active: Day and Night

Sex diff: Males larger with horns
Habitat: Riverine canopy woodland, always near water
Food: Medium grasses
Soc. Org: Harem herds of ± 6 females and one dominant male, territorial, satellite males

E: Defassa Waterbuck Sw: Kuru

117

The large Antelopes continued

E: Coke's Hartebeest   Sw: Kongoni

Coke's Hartebeest *(Alcelaphus buselaphus cokei)*
Sw: Kongoni **Ger:** Kuhantilope **Fr:** Le Bubale

Height: 132cm
Weight: M 170kg; F 150kg
Gestation: 8 months
Litter: One
Life span: 19 years
Active: Mainly diurnal

Sex diff: Males slightly larger
Habitat: Bounderies of grassy plains and woodland
Food: Grass, non-selective
Soc. Org: Harem troops

E: White-bearded Gnu Sw: Nyumbu ya montu

White-bearded Gnu *(Connochaetes taurinus)*
Sw: Nyumbu ya montu **Ger:** Weissbart **Fr:** Le Gnou Bleu

Height: M 150cm; F 135cm
Weight: M 250kg; F 200kg
Gestation: 8,5 months
Litter: One
Life span: 20 years
Active: Mainly diurnal

Sex diff: Males larger
Habitat: Short grass plains, open woodland
Food: Grass, preferably short grass
Soc. Org: Gregarious, one bull and several females, territorial during rut

E: Topi   Sw: Nyamera topi

Topi *(Damaliscus lunatis topi)*
Sw: Nyamera topi **Ger:** Leierantilope **Fr:** Damalisque

Height: 125cm
Weight: M 140kg; F 110kg
Gestation: 7,5 - 8 months
Litter: One
Life span: 12 - 15 years
Active: Mainly diurnal

Sex diff: Males larger
Habitat: Seasonally flooded grassland in dry regions
Food: Tall floodplain grasses
Soc. Org: Small harems with one male, territorial

Topi female with young

ANIMALS – MAMMALS

The middle-sized Antelopes

Grant's Gazelle *(Gazella granti)*
Sw: Swala Granti **Ger:** Grantgazelle **Fr:** La Gazelle de Grant

Height: M 90cm; F 83cm
Weight: M 70kg; F 50kg
Gestation: 6,5 months
Litter: One
Life span: 12 years
Active: Mainly diurnal
Sex diff: Males larger, thicker horns

Habitat: Arid areas, open grass plains with bush
Food: Grass and leaves, not water dependent
Soc. Org: Dominant male with 10 - 30 females, bachelor herds, territorial

E: Grant's Gazelle   Sw: Swala Granti

Thomson's Gazelle *(Gazella rufifrons thomsoni)*
Sw: Swala Tomi **Ger:** Thomsongazella **Fr:** La Gazella de Thomson

Height: M 62cm; F 55cm
Weight: M 28kg; F 20kg
Gestation: 6 months
Litter: One
Life span: 10 years
Active: Mainly diurnal

Sex diff: Males larger, thicker and longer horns
Habitat: Open, short grass plains
Food: Short grass and about 10% foliage, water dependent
Soc. Org: Loose, one male, up to 60 females, bachelor herds

E: Thomson's Gazelle   Sw: Swala Tomi

Impala *(Aepyceros melampus)*
Sw: Swala Pala **Ger:** Schwartzfersenantilope **Fr:** Le Pallah

Height: M 90cm; F 86cm
Weight: M 65kg; F 50kg
Gestation: 6,5 months
Litter: One
Life span: 12 years
Active: Mainly diurnal

Sex diff: Males have horns, larger than females
Habitat: Open woodland, water
Food: Grass and leaves
Soc. Org: Gregarious, dominant male, territorial during rut

E: Impala   Sw: Swala Pala

Bohor Reedbuck *(Redunca redunca)*
Sw: Tohe **Ger:** Gemeiner Riedbock **Fr:** Le Redunca

Height: M 75cm; F 70cm
Weight: M 55kg; F 45kg
Gestation: 7 - 7,5 months
Litter: One
Life span: 10 years
Active: Day and Night

Sex diff: Males have horns
Habitat: Swampy areas
Food: Tough grasses that grow in swampy areas, water dependent
Soc. Org: Solitary, pairs or troops, territorial

E: Bohor Reedbuck   Sw: Tohe

ANIMALS – MAMMALS

119

Mammal check list

The middle-sized Antelopes continued

E: Mountain Reedbuck   Sw: Tohe ya milima

Mountain Reedbuck *(Redunca fulvorufula)*
Sw: Tohe ya milima   **Ger:** Bergriedbock   **Fr:** Le redunca de Montagne

Height: 73cm	**Sex diff:** Males have horns
Weight: M 30kg; F 25kg	**Habitat:** Grass ridges in
Gestation: 8 months	mountains with water
Litter: One	**Food:** Tough grasses
Life span: 11 years	**Soc Org:** Gregarious, groups
Active: Day and night	of 3 - 6

E: Bushbuck   Sw: Pango/Mbawala

Bushbuck *(Tragelaphus scriptus)*
Sw: Pango/Mbawala   **Ger:** Schirrantilope   **Fr:** L'Antilope harnaché, Le Guib

Height: M 90cm; F 75cm	**Sex diff:** Males have horns
Weight: M 60kg; F 44kg	**Habitat:** Riverine woodland,
Gestation: 6 months	dense bush
Litter: One	**Food:** Leaves, fruit
Life span: 11 years	**Soc. Org:** Pairs or family groups,
Active: Day and night	mostly solitary, non-territorial

E: Oribi   Sw: Taya

Oribi *(Ourebia ourebi)*
Sw: Taya   **Ger:** Bleichböckchen   **Fr:** L'Ourébie

Height: ± 58cm	**Sex diff:** Males have horns,
Weight: M 15kg; F 17kg	female larger
Gestation: 7 months	**Habitat:** Open grassveld
Litter: One	**Food:** Grass maintained by fire
Life span: 13 years	**Soc. Org:** Solitary or small
Active: Mainly diurnal	groups, territorial

The dwarf Antelopes

E: Klipspringer   Sw: Ngurunguru/Mbuzi mawe

Klipspringer *(Oreotragus oreotragus)*
Sw: Ngurunguru/Mbuzi mawe   **Ger:** Klippspringer   **Fr:** L'Oréotrague

Height: 52cm	**Sex diff:** Males have horns
Weight: M 12kg; F 14kg	**Habitat:** Rocky outcrops,
Gestation: 7,5 months	mountains and kopjes
Litter: One	**Food:** Leaves, fruit, herbs, shrubs
Life span: 7 years	**Soc. Org:** Pairs or family groups,
Active: Day and night	territorial

The dwarf Antelopes continued

Steinbok *(Raphicerus campestris)*
Sw: Dondor/Isha **Ger:** Steinböckchen **Fr:** Le Steenbok

Height: 52cm
Weight: ± 11kg
Gestation: 6 months
Litter: One, sometimes two
Life span: 7 years
Active: Day and night

Sex diff: Males have horns
Habitat: Arid, unstable areas
Food: Grass, leaves, fruit, bulbs, not water dependent
Soc. Org: Solitary, pairs or mother and young, territorial

E: Steinbok   Sw: Dondor/Isha

Bush Duiker *(Sylvicapra grimmia)*
Sw: Nsya **Ger:** Kronenducker **Fr:** Le Cephalophe couronné

Height: ± 57cm
Weight: M 15kg; F 18kg
Gestation: 6 months
Litter: One
Life span: 12 years
Active: Day and night

Sex diff: Males have horns
Habitat: Varied, woodland with enough cover
Food: Leaves, herbage
Soc. Org: Solitary or pairs, territorial

SAN PARKS

E: Bush Duiker   Sw: Nsya

Blue Duiker *(Philantomba monticola)*
Sw: Ndimba/Chesi **Ger:** Blauducker **Fr:** Le Céphalophe bleu

Height: ± 35cm
Weight: M 4,7kg; F 6kg
Gestation: ± 4 months
Litter: One
Life span: ± 10 years
Active: Day and night

Sex diff: Both have horns, smaller or sometimes absent in females
Habitat: Forests
Food: Leaves, fruit
Soc. Org: Solitary or pairs, territorial

Burge Cillié

E: Blue Duiker   Sw: Ndimba/Chesi

Kirk's Dik-dik *(Madoqua kirkii)*
Sw: Dikidiki/Suguya **Ger:** Kirkdikdik **Fr:** Le Dik-dik de kirk

Height: 39cm
Weight: 5kg
Gestation: 5,5 - 6 months
Litter: One
Life span: 9 years
Active: Day and night

Sex diff: Males have horns
Habitat: Thick woodland
Food: Leaves, fruit, not water dependent
Soc. Org: Solitary or pairs, territorial

Male

E: Kirk's Dik-dik   Sw: Dikidiki/Suguya

ANIMALS - MAMMALS

121

ANIMALS - MAMMALS

E: Olive Baboon   Sw: Nyani

Olive Baboon *(Papio anubis)*
Sw: Nyani **Ger:** Anubispaviaan **Fr:** Le Babouin doguer

Height: M 65cm; F 55cm
Weight: M 28kg; F 17kg
Gestation: 6 months
Litter: One
Life span: 30 - 40 years
Active: Diurnal

Sex diff: Males larger
Habitat: Woodland savannah and mountain areas
Food: Fruit, berries, insects, sometimes meat
Soc. Org: Troops of ± 70

E: Black-faced Vervet Monkey   Sw: Tumbili /Ngedere

Black-faced Vervet Monkey *(Cercopithecus aethiops)*
Sw: Tumbili /Ngedere **Ger:** Grünmeerkatze **Fr:** Le grivet

Height: M 45cm, F 80cm
Weight: M 7kg; F 5,5kg
Gestation: 6.5 months
Litter: One
Life span: 24 years
Active: Diurnal
Sex diff: Males larger, blue & red genitals

Habitat: Savannah & bush, riverine forest
Food: Fruit, berries, flowers, bark, insects, nestlings, small mammals
Soc. Org: Organised troops of 6 - 30, one dominant male

SAN PARKS

E: Lesser Bushbaby Sw: Komba ya Senegal

Lesser Bushbaby *(Galago senegalensis subsp. braccatus)*
Sw: Komba ya Senegal **Ger:** Senegalgalago **Fr:** Galago du Sénégal

Height: 17,5cm
Weight: 150 - 250g
Gestation: 4 months
Litter: 1 - 2
Active: Nocturnal
Life span: 10 years

Sex diff: None
Habitat: Acacia woodland
Food: Gum, grasshoppers, moths, spiders
Soc. Org: Gregarious, territorial

SAN PARKS

E: Greater Bushbaby Sw: Komba Miombo

Greater Bushbaby *(Otolemur/Galago crassicaudatus)*
Sw: Komba ya Miombo **Ger:** Riesengalago **Fr:** Le Galago à queue épaisse

Height: 37 cm
Weight: M 1,22 kg; F 1,13 kg
Gestation: 4 months
Litter: 1 - 2
Active: Nocturnal
Life span: 14 years

Sex diff: Males slightly larger
Habitat: Woodland and forest, especially Miombo woodland
Food: Fruit, gum, insects, birds
Soc. Org: Partly solitary, family groups sleep together, territorial

Mammal check list

Tree Hyrax *(Dendrohyrax arboreus)*
Sw: Perere **Ger:** Waldschliefer **Fr:** L daman d'arbre

Length: 40 - 60cm
Weight: M 3,5kg; F 2,4kg
Gestation: 8 months
Litter: 1-2
Life span: 12 years
Active: Nocturnal

Sex diff: None
Habitat: Mountains, moist savannah forest
Food: Leaves, fruit, herbage, grass, insects, eggs, lizards
Soc. Org: Usually in pairs with young or solitary, territorial

E: Tree Hyrax   Sw: Perere

Rock Hyrax *(Heterohyrax brucei)*
Sw: Pimbi **Ger:** Steppenschliefer **Fr:** Le daman de steppe

Length: 40 - 57cm
Weight: M 2,75kg; F 2,5kg
Gestation: 8 months
Litter: 1-2
Life span: 12 years
Active: Diurnal

Sex diff: None
Habitat: Plains to mountains, kopjes, savannah
Food: Mostly leaves, also herbage and grass
Soc. Org: Usually in pairs with young or solitary, territorial

E: Rock Hyrax   Sw: Pimbi

Red Rock Hare *(Pronolagus sp.)*
Sw: Sungura **Ger:** Rothase **Fr:** Le Lièvre roux

Length: 43 - 53cm
Weight: 1,3 - 2,5kg
Gestation: 4 weeks
Litter: 1 - 2
Life span: Not known
Active: Nocturnal

Sex diff: None
Habitat: Rocky areas with bush cover like cliffs
Food: Grass and herbage
Soc. Org: Small groups or solitary, forage alone

SAN PARKS

E: Red Rock Hare   Sw: Sungura

Cape Hare *(Lepus capensis)*
Sw: Sungura **Ger:** Kaphase **Fr:** Le Lièvre du Cap

Length: 45 -75cm
Weight: M 1,6kg; F 1,9kg
Gestation: 5 weeks
Litter: 1 - 3
Life span: 5 years
Active: Nocturnal

Sex diff: Females slightly larger
Habitat: Open grassland with patches of tall grass
Food: Short grass, herbs
Soc. Org: Solitary, tolerates neighbours

SAN PARKS

E: Cape Hare Sw: Sungura

ANIMALS – MAMMALS

123

Mongooses

E: Dwarf Mongoose   Sw: Kitafe

Dwarf Mongoose *(Helogale parvula)*
Sw: Kitafe **Ger:** Zwergichneumon **Fr:** La Mangouste nain

Length: 18 - 28cm
Weight: ± 280g
Gestation: 8 weeks
Litter: 2 - 4
Life span: ± 6 years
Active: Diurnal

Sex diff: None
Habitat: Thickets and woodland with termitaria
Food: Termites, worms, snails, insects
Soc. Org: Form colonies of 10 or more

E: Slender Mongoose   Sw: Nguchiro

Slender Mongoose *(Galerella sanguinea)*
Sw: Nguchiro **Ger:** Schlankichneumon **Fr:** La Mangouste rouge

Length: 25 - 40cm
Weight: M 400-900g; F 350-500g
Gestation: Not known
Litter: 1 - 2
Life span: ± 8 years
Active: Diurnal

Sex diff: None
Habitat: Varies from desert to rainforest, very adaptable
Food: Termites, beetles, locusts, insects, eggs, mice
Soc. Org: Solitary

SAN PARKS

E: White-tailed Mongoose Sw: Karambago

White-tailed Mongoose *(Ichneumia albicauda)*
Sw: Karambago **Ger:** Weisschwanzichneumon
Fr: La Mangouste à queu blanche

Length: ± 60cm
Weight: M 4,5kg; F 3,5kg
Gestation: Not known
Litter: 1 - 3
Life span: 12,5 years
Active: Nocturnal

Sex diff: Male slightly heavier
Habitat: Woodlands with plenty water, along rivers
Food: Insects, mice, frogs, birds, snails, fruit
Soc. Org: Solitary or pairs

E: Banded Mongoose   Sw: Nkuchiro

Banded Mongoose *(Mungos mungo)*
Sw: Nkuchiro **Ger:** Zebramanguste **Fr:** La Mangue rayée

Length: 30-45cm
Weight: 1,5 - 2,2kg
Gestation: 8 weeks
Litter: 2 - 8
Life span: ± 8 years
Active: Diurnal

Sex diff: None
Habitat: Riverine forest or dense thornveld
Food: Insects, reptiles, eggs, fruit, snails
Soc. Org: Gregarious, colonies of 30 or more

ANIMALS - MAMMALS

Mammal check list

Mongooses continued

Water / Marsh Mongoose *(Atilax paludinosus)*
Sw: Nguchiro wa maji **Ger:** Sumpfichneumon **Fr:** La Mangouste des arais

Length: 45 - 60cm	**Sex diff:** None
Weight: 2 - 4kg	**Habitat:** Riverine, swamps, dams
Gestation: Not known	**Food:** Frogs, crabs, mice, fish,
Litter: 1 - 3	insects
Life span: 11 years	**Soc. Org:** Solitary
Active: Nocturnal	

E: Water / Marsh Mongoose   Sw: Nguchiro wa maji

Other small mammals

Antbear / Aardvark *(Orycteropus afer)*
Sw: Muhanga/Kukukifuku **Ger:** Erdferkel **Fr:** Le Orycterope

Height: 61cm	**Sex diff:** Males slightly larger
Weight: M 70kg; F 50kg	**Habitat:** Very adaptable
Gestation: 7 months	**Food:** Termites and ant
Litter: One	**Soc. Org:** Solitary
Life span: 18 years	
Active: Nocturnal	

E: Antbear / Aardvark   Sw: Muhanga / Kukukifuku

Pangolin (Manis temmincki)
Sw: Kaka/Kakakuona **Ger:** Steppenschuppentier
Fr: Pangolin de Temminck

Length: 81cm	**Sex diff:** None
Weight: 4,5 - 14,5 kg	**Habitat:** Sandy soil in dry
Gestation: 4,5 months	bushveld
Litter: One	**Food:** Termites and ant
Life span: 12 years	**Soc. Org:** Solitary
Active: Nocturnal	

E: Pangolin   Sw: Kakakuona

Porcupine *(Hystrix africaeaustralis)*
Sw: Nungu **Ger:** Südafrika-Stachelschwein
Fr: Le Porc-épique de l'Afrique du Sud

Length: 84cm	**Sex diff:** Females heavier
Weight: 20 - 25kg	**Habitat:** Woodland and scrub
Gestation: 3 months	**Food:** Roots, bulbs, rhizomes,
Litter: 1 - 4	vegetables, fruit
Life span: 8 years	**Soc. Org:** Loose groups of
Active: Nocturnal	± 4

E: Porcupine   Sw: Nungu

ANIMALS – MAMMALS

E: Spring Hare   Sw: Kamendegere

SAN PARKS

E: Greater Canerat   Sw: Ndezi / Nkungusi

SAN PARKS

E: Clawless Otter Sw: Fisi maji

E: Honey Badger Sw: Nyegere/Kinyegale

Spring Hare *(Pedetes capensis)*
Sw: Kamendegere **Ger:** Springhase **Fr:** Le Lièrre sauteur

Length: 40cm + tail 40cm
Weight: 2,5 - 3,8kg
Gestation: 2 months
Litter: One
Life span: 7 years
Active: Nocturnal

Sex diff: None
Habitat: Near pans or higher, ground in sandy-loam soil
Food: Rhizomes, tubers, grass
Soc. Org: Solitary, or pair with young

Greater Canerat *(Thryonomys swinderianus)*
Sw: Ndezi/Nkungusi **Ger:** Grosse Rohrratte **Fr:** L'Aulacode grand

Length: 50 - 60cm
Weight: 4,5 - 9kg
Gestation: 3 months
Litter: 2 - 6
Life span: 4 years
Active: Nocturnal

Sex diff: None
Habitat: Dense grass, reed beds, sedges, swamps
Food: Roots, shoots, grass stems, reeds
Soc. Org: Groups up to 12

Clawless Otter *(Aonyx capensis)*
Sw: Fisi maji **Ger:** Kapfingerotter **Fr:** La Loutre a joues blanches

Length: 80cm + tail 50cm
Weight: 15 - 22kg
Gestation: 9 months
Litter: One, rarely 2
Life span: 15 years
Active: Diurnal

Sex diff: None
Habitat: Aquatic
Food: Frogs, crabs, fish, birds, reptiles, insects
Soc. Org: Solitary or pairs, mother and baby

Honey Badger *(Mellivora capensis)*
Sw: Nyegere/Kinyegale **Ger:** Honigdachs **Fr:** Le Ratel

Height: 70cm + tail 20cm
Weight: 10 - 16kg
Gestation: 6,5 months
Litter: Usually 2
Life span: 24 years
Active: Nocturnal

Sex diff: Males are heavier
Habitat: Most habitats except true deserts
Food: Honey, fruit, birds, scorpions, reptiles
Soc. Org: Usually solitary, rarely pairs

Striped Polecat / Zorilla *(Ictonyx striata)*
Sw: Kicheche/Kanu **Ger:** Streifeniltis **Fr:** Le Zorille commun

Length: 33cm + tail 25cm
Weight: 650 - 1 300g
Gestation: 5 weeks
Litter: 2-3
Life span: 5,5 years
Active: Nocturnal

Sex diff: Males larger
Habitat: Rock crevices, under piles of stones
Food: Small mammals, birds, eggs, reptiles, insects
Soc. Org: Solitary

E: Striped Polecat / Zorilla Sw: Kicheche/Kanu

African Civet *(Civettictis civetta)*
Sw: Fungo/Ngawa **Ger:** Afrika-Zibetkatze **Fr:** La Civette dé Afrique

Height: 40cm
Weight: M 11,4kg; F 14,9kg
Gestation: 2 months
Litter: 1-4
Life span: 12 years
Active: Nocturnal

Sex diff: Females larger
Habitat: Bushveld with thick undergrowth
Food: Insects, mice, fruit, reptiles and birds
Soc. Org: Solitary

E: African Civet   Sw: Fungo / Ngawa

Large-spotted Genet *(Genetta tigrina)*
Sw: Kanu **Ger:** Grossfleckginsterkatze **Fr:** La genetta à grandes taches

Length: ± 45cm + tail 45cm
Weight: 1 - 3kg
Gestation: 2 months
Litter: One
Life span: 13 years
Active: Nocturnal

Sex diff: None
Habitat: Bush with plenty water
Food: Rodents, insects, birds, crabs
Soc. Org: Solitary or in pairs

E: Large-spotted Genet   Sw: Kanu

Small-spotted Genet *(Genetta genetta)*
Sw: Kanu **Ger:** Gemeine Ginsterkatze **Fr:** La Genette vulgaire

Height: 15 - 20cm
Weight: M 2,5kg; F 1,7kg
Gestation: 2 months
Litter: 1-4
Life span: 15 years
Active: Nocturnal

Sex diff: None
Habitat: Open dry savannah with sufficient cover
Food: Small mammals, birds, snails, fruit, crabs
Soc. Org: Solitary

E: Small-spotted Genet Sw: Kanu

ANIMALS – MAMMALS

Other small mammals continued

E: Hedgehog   Sw: Kalungujeje

Hedgehog *(Erinaceus albiventris)*
Sw: Kalungujeje **Ger:** Weisbauchigel **Fr:** Le Hérisson à ventre blanc

Length: 17 - 23cm	**Sex diff:** None
Weight: 500 - 700g	**Habitat:** Woodland, bushland, grassland
Gestation: 5,5 weeks	
Litter: 2 - 10, usually 5	**Food:** Earthworms, insects, snails, lizards, frogs, carrion, fungi, roots
Life span: 8 - 10 years	
Active: Nocturnal	**Soc. Org:** Solitary, except mother with young

Rats, Mice, Gerbils & Shrews

E: Woodland Dormouse Sw: Panya miti

Woodland Dormouse *(Graphiurus murinus)*
Sw: Panya miti

Length: 80 - 110mm	**Habitat:** Woodland, arboreal, beehives
Weight: 40 - 85g	
Litter size: 4	**Food:** Dead bees, honey, wax, bagworms, termites
Gestation: 24 days	
Active: Nocturnal	

E: Water Rat Sw: Panya

Water Rat *(Dasymys incomtus)*
Sw: Panya

Length: ± 155mm	**Habitat:** Swamps, reedbeds, Riverine vegetation
Weight: 90 - 120g	
Litter: 1 - 3	**Food:** Mostly vegetarian, insects
Gestation: Not known	
Active: Nocturnal	

E: Pencil-tailed Tree Rat   Sw: Panya

Pencil-tailed Tree Rat *(Thallomys paedulcus)*
Sw: Panya

Length: 140 - 150mm	**Habitat:** Mainly Acacia trees
Weight: 100 - 120g	**Food:** Mainly *Acacia* seeds, pods and leaves
Litter: Not known	
Gestation: Not known	
Active: At night	

ANIMALS – MAMMALS

SAN PARKS

Bush Rat / Red Veld Rat *(Aethomys chrysophilus)*
Sw: Panya

Length: 125-150mm
Weight: 82 - 110g
Litter: 27
Gestation: ± 22 days
Active: Nocturnal

Habitat: Grassland with scrub
Food: Grass seeds, nuts of fruit

E: Bush Rat / Red Veld Rat   Sw: Panya

Four-striped Ground Mouse *(Rhabdomys pumilio)*
Sw: Panya

Length: 100 - 120mm
Weight: 42 - 52g
Litter: 3 - 9
Gestation: ± 25 days
Active: Diurnal

Habitat: Varied, prefers grassland
Food: Omnivorous

E: Four-striped Ground Mouse   Sw: Panya

Single-striped Mouse *(Lemniscomys griselda)*
Sw: Panya

Length: 130 - 150mm
Weight: 44 - 80g
Litter: 5-7
Gestation: Not known
Active: Diurnal

Habitat: Grassland in low Acacia veld
Food: Mainly grass seeds, vegetable matter

E: Single-striped Mouse   Sw: Panya

Shamba Rat/Mutlimammate Mouse *(Praomys natalensis)*
Sw: Panya

Length: 120 - 140mm
Weight: 50 - 60g
Litter: 10 - 16, up to 24
Gestation: ± 23 days
Active: Nocturnal

Habitat: Very adaptable, mostly in woodlands
Food: Acacia seeds, pods, fruit, grass

E: Shamba Rat Sw: Panya

ANIMALS – MAMMALS

129

ANIMALS - MAMMALS

E: Pouched Mouse   Sw: Panya

Pouched Mouse *(Saccostomus campestris)*
Sw: Panya

Length: ± 160mm
Weight: 42 - 48g
Litter: ± 3 - 5
Gestation: 20 - 21 days
Active: Nocturnal, solitary

Habitat: Varied, prefers sandy woodland
Food: Mainly seeds of shrubs and trees like *Acacia*

E: Chestnut Climbing Mouse   Sw: Panya

Chestnut Climbing Mouse *(Dendromus mystacalis)*
Sw: Panya

Length: 60 - 80mm
Weight: 7 - 14g
Litter: 3 - 5
Gestation: Not known
Active: Nocturnal

Habitat: Arboreal at low altitudes
Food: Grains and insects

E: Grey Pygmy Climbing Mouse S: Panya

Grey Pygmy Climbing Mouse *(Dendromus melanotis)*
Sw: Panya

Length: 56 - 81mm
Weight: 4 - 12g
Litter: 3 - 5
Gestation: Not known
Active: Nocturnal

Habitat: Arboreal at low altitudes
Food: Grains and insects

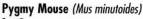
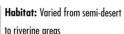

E: Pygmy Mouse Sw: Panya

Pygmy Mouse *(Mus minutoides)*
Sw: Panya

Length: 53 - 70mm
Weight: 6 - 11g
Litter: ± 4
Gestation: ± 19 days
Active: Nocturnal

Habitat: Varied from semi-desert to riverine areas
Food: Omnivorous

Rats, Mice, Gerbils & Shrews continued

Bushveld Gerbil *(Tatera leucogaster)*
Sw: Panya

Length: 120 - 160mm
Weight: 60 - 125g
Litter: 4 - 5
Gestation: Not known
Active: Nocturnal

Habitat: Well-drained, sandy areas, sub-Saharan areas
Food: Seeds, stems, roots, insects

E: Bushveld Gerbil   Sw: Panya

Lesser Elephant Shrew *(Elephantulus brachyrynchus)*
Sw: Sange **Ger:** Elephantenspitzmaus **Fr:** Macroscélide

Length: 210 - 280mm
Weight: 25 - 70g
Litter: 1 - 2
Gestation: ± 2 months
Active: Diurnal

Habitat: Dry scrubby bush
Food: Invertebrates

E: Lesser Elephant Shrew   Sw: Sange

Lesser Red Musk Shrew *(Crocidura hirta)*
Sw: Kirukanjia

Length: 115 - 160mm
Weight: 8 - 22g
Litter: 3 - 4
Gestation: 18 days
Active: Nocturnal

Habitat: Damp areas along streams
Food: Earthworms, insects, termites

E: Lesser Red Musk Shrew Sw: Kirukanjia

Bats

Epauletted Fruit Bat *(Epomophorus sp.)*
Sw: Popo

Length: 120 - 160mm
Weight: 64 - 140g
Litter: One, seldom twins
Gestation: Not known
Active: Nocturnal

Habitat: Fruit-bearing trees, riverine vegetation
Food: Wild figs, marula and all other wild fruit
Soc. Org: Gregarious

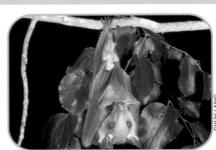

E: Epauletted Fruit Bat S: Popo

ANIMALS - MAMMALS

ANIMALS – MAMMALS

E: Common Slit-faced Bat   Sw: Popo

Common Slit-faced Bat *(Nycteris thebaica)*
Sw: Popo

Length: 92 - 120mm
Weight: 7 - 15g
Litter: One
Gestation: 5 months
Active: Nocturnal

Habitat: Open savannah and dense coastal forests
Food: Crickets, grasshoppers gleaned from branches and ground
Soc. Org: Gregarious - colonies

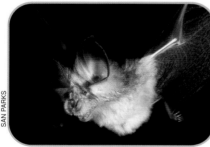

E: Yellow House Bat   Sw: Popo

Yellow House Bat *(Scotophilus dinganii)*
Sw: Popo

Length: 123 - 14mm
Weight: 22 - 37g
Litter: 1 - 3
Gestation: Not known
Active: Nocturnal

Habitat: Savannah woodlands, lower altitudes
Food: Aerial insect feeder, bugs, flies, moths
Soc. Org: Gregarious - up to 12

Darling's Horseshoe Bat *(Rhinolophus darlingi)*
Sw: Popo

Length: 80 - 90mm
Weight: 8 - 10g
Litter: 1 - 2
Gestation: Not known
Active: Nocturnal

Habitat: Savannah woodland, rocky terrain
Food: Insects
Soc. Org: Colonies of a few dozen

E: Darling's Horseshoe Bat   Sw: Popo

Hildebrandt's Horseshoe Bat *(Rhinolophus hildebrandtii)*
Sw: Popo

Length: 108 - 125mm
Weight: 26 - 32g
Litter: Not known
Gestation: Not known
Active: Nocturnal

Habitat: Savannah woodland
Food: Insects - aerial foragers in dense clutter
Soc. Org: Gregarious, colonies of a few hundred

E: Hildebrandt's Horseshoe Bat   Sw: Popo

SAN PARKS

Little Free-tailed Bat *(Chaerephon pumilis)*
Sw: Popo

Length: 70 - 120mm
Weight: 10 - 16g
Litter: One
Gestation: Not known
Active: Nocturnal

Habitat: Varied, savannah, mountains, arid
Food: Bugs, beetles, moths, aerial feeders
Soc. Org: Gregarious

E: Little Free-tailed Bat   Sw: Popo

Angolan Free-tailed Bat *(Mops condylurus)*
Sw: Popo

Length: 110 - 125mm
Weight: 16 - 22g
Litter: One
Gestation: 58 days
Active: Nocturnal

Habitat: Varied, not in deserts
Food: Beetles, high aerial feeders (strong jaws)
Soc. Org: Gregarious

E: Angolan Free-tailed Bat   Sw: Popo

Schlieffen's Bat *(Nycticeius schlieffeni)*
Sw: Popo

Length: 65 - 80mm
Weight: 3,7 - 5,0g
Litter: 1 - 3
Gestation: 11 weeks
Active: Nocturnal

Habitat: Savannah woodland, riparian, near pans
Food: Beetles, lacewings, flies, moths, bugs
Soc. Org: Solitary

E: Schlieffen's Bat   Sw: Popo

ANIMALS – MAMMALS

SAN PARKS

Baboon mother and baby

REPTILES AND AMPHIBIANS

Agama Lizard (Agama agama)

REPTILES AND AMPHIBIANS

INTRODUCTION TO REPTILES

This section will provide just a few photographic examples of the main groups of reptiles to give an understanding of the group as a whole. Hopefully it will also stimulate an interest in this fascinating group regarded by most people as 'less than charming'.

The most obvious characteristic of reptiles is their dry, horny skin that is usually modified into scales. The scales prevent water loss through the skin. Other differences to mammals is that they have a single occipital condyle (knob at the back of the skull) where mammals have two. They have a single bone in the ear, instead of the three found in mammals. Unlike mammals, each half of the lower jaw consists of several bones. Reptiles are cold-blooded. This term is confusing since their blood temperature is often higher than that of mammals. 'Cold-blooded' simply means that they obtain their heat externally, mostly from the sun. They regulate their body temperature by moving between sun and shade, in many cases from above ground to under ground. Mammals generate their heat internally by metabolising food. Reptiles have the ability to become temporarily dormant during cold weather and can survive and grow on much less food than mammals.

The first reptiles occurred about 315 million years ago and for about 150 million years the dinosaurs and their relatives dominated the earth, more specifically during the Jurassic era between 190 million to 130 million years ago (Branch, 1996).

The following groups will be briefly dealt with:
- Crocodiles
- Snakes
- Lizards and Chameleons
- Tortoises and Terrapins

NILE CROCODILE

Crocodiles have changed very little during the last 65 million years. There are 12 living species left throughout the tropical regions of the world. The Nile Crocodile (*Crocodylus niloticus*) is the most common in Africa but in west and central Africa, the African Slender-snouted Crocodile (*Crododylus cataphractus*) can also be found.

Anatomy   The average Nile Crocodile is about 2,5m to 3,5m long and the maximum length is about 5,9m. They rarely weigh over 1 000kg and may live for as long as 100 years. Their eyes and nostrils are situated on top of the head to afford them vision and breathing whilst submerged. When a crocodile feeds under water, the breathing passages are closed at the back of the mouth by means of a flap, called a 'gular flap'. The nostrils are also flapped for the same purpose. Crocodiles open their mouths to regulate their body temperature. The air-flow causes the blood near the soft surface of the mouth to to cool down and to spread to the rest of the body.

Breeding   They become sexually mature at about 12 to 15 years of age. There is a dominant hierarchy amongst males, usually determined by size. Mating takes place in the water.

Nile Crocodile (Crocodylus niloticus) opening its mouth to regulate its body temperature

Crocodiles and Snakes

Nesting The female Crocodile selects a sand bank in the open sun above the flood level, with cover nearby, to lay her eggs. She digs a hole of ±40cm deep with her hind legs and lays about 20 to 80 eggs. The female guards the nest and does not eat during incubation.

The male also remains in the vicinity but is not allowed at the actual nest. The sex of the hatchlings depends on the egg incubation temperatures. Females develop at lower temperatures and males at higher temperatures. After about three months (85 to 90 days) the hatchlings emit a shrill, high-pitched sound whilst still in the eggs. This is the sign for the female to carefully open the nest after which she takes them all into her mouth. The hatchlings are ±30cm long. She carefully takes them to the water and gently releases them. They remain in the general vicinity for six to eight weeks, feeding mainly on small aquatic fauna. The mother does not provide any postnatal care, and as they are caught by large water birds and other predators, the mortality rate during this time is very high.

A Crocodile hatchling (±30cm long)

Snake check list

Snakes probably evolved from legless lizards. Their eyes lack eyelids, they have no external ears, the tongue is retractile and can be withdrawn into a sheath. They have long backbones of up to 440 vertebrae and many ribs that are used for locomotion and to maintain body shape. They are all carnivorous. In many species the lower jaw can be dislocated to swallow large prey. They regularly shed their skin, usually in one piece, starting at the nose (Bill Branch, 1996). Only a few species of snake can shed their tail but they do not have the ability to regenerate a new one.

Mozambique Spitting Cobra (Naje mossambica)

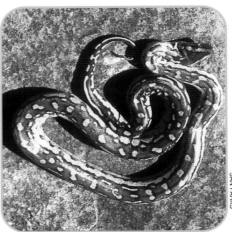

African Rock Python (Python sebae)

Snake check list continued

Black Mamba (Dendroaspis polylepus)

Egyptian Cobra (Naje haje)

Puff Adder (Bitis arietans)

Rhombic Night Adder (Causus rhombeatus)

Tree Snake or Boomslang (Dispholidus typus)

Spotted Bush Snake (Philothamnus semivariegatus)

Shield-nosed Snake (Aspidelaps scutatus)

Sand Snake (Psammophis sp.)

REPTILES AND AMPHIBIANS

Venomous Snakes of Africa Of the ±2 000 species of snakes found in the world, only 300 are dangerous to man and very few will attack if not threatened. Of these, about 50 are marine

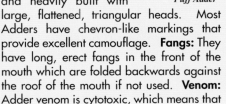

African Rock Python

and therefore seldom encountered. Only 14 African snakes have been recorded to have caused deaths. They are the Puff Adder, the Gaboon Adder, the Black Mamba, the Green Mamba, the five Cobras (Cape Cobra, Egyptian Cobra, Mozambique Spitting Cobra, Black Spitting Cobra and the Western Barred Cobra), the Namibian Coral Snake, the Rinkhals, the Boomslang, the Bird Snake and the African Rock Python. The Rock Python is not poisonous but kills by constricting and swallowing its prey whole. See pg 141 for more details on pythons.

The number of snakebite deaths are insignificant compared to other causes of death. People are generally terrified of snakes but snakes will only attack when cornered. They occupy a vital niche in the food chain and are extremely important in vermin control as they feed mainly on rodents.

Snake venom: Snake venom is produced by the salivary glands and has evolved from normal digestive enzymes, not unlike the enzymes found in human saliva. In venomous snakes the salivary gland has been modified to form a venom gland, which is called Duvernoy's gland in some groups. A complex muscle and duct system causes venom to ooze into the hollow, syringe-like fangs on voluntary contraction. The amount of venom injected is predetermined and depends on the size of prey or how threatened a snake feels.

Fangs: Fang replacement occurs at intervals throughout the life of the snake. The poisonous snakes can be divided into front-fanged and back-fanged snakes. The venom of front-fanged snakes is **cytotoxic**, which means it affects the body tissue (Adders), and **neurotoxic**, which means it affects the nervous system (Mambas and Cobras). The venom of back-fanged snakes is **haemotoxic**, affecting the blood circulation by preventing blood-clotting (Tree Snake/Boomslang and Vine Snake). The following snakes occuring in Tanzania are considered deadly: The Black Mamba, the Puff Adder, the Night Adder, the Egyptian Cobra, the Mozambique Spitting Cobra, the Tree Snake and the Vine Snake.

**ADDERS Genus Bitis
(Cytotoxic venom)**

Puff Adder

Body shape: Typical Adders are short, thick and heavily built with large, flattened, triangular heads. Most Adders have chevron-like markings that provide excellent camouflage. **Fangs:** They have long, erect fangs in the front of the mouth which are folded backwards against the roof of the mouth if not used. **Venom:** Adder venom is cytotoxic, which means that

it destroys cellular tissue. It spreads mainly through the lymphatic system. The Puff Adder (*Bitis arietans*) has the distinction of causing more bites of a serious nature than all the other venomous snakes combined. The venom is slow-acting and, in a serious case, death will only occur after 24 hours or more. Less than 5% of bites have proved to be fatal.

Front Fangs of Adders

R
E
P
T
I
L
E
S

A
N
D

A
M
P
H
I
B
I
A
N
S

139

REPTILES AND AMPHIBIANS

MAMBAS: Genus Dendroaspis (Neurotoxic venom)

Body shape: The Black Mamba (*Dendroaspis polylepis*) is a shy snake and will not attack if not cornered, but it is extremely agile and can strike from 1,5m to 1,8m away. Although the Black Mamba is the deadliest snake in Africa, it is only responsible for a small percentage of snakebite fatalities. They are usually olive-brown with a diagnostic coffin-shaped head - in other words, the head is broad behind the eyes with a long snout. They have relatively small eyes and the inside of the mouth is black, hence the common name of 'Black Mamba'. **Fangs:** The fang sheaths are bulbous and situated between the tip of the snout and the eye. **Venom:** The venom is neurotoxic, which means that it affects the nerves. It is rapidly spread by venous blood, therefore the clinical effect is distant from the bite, but almost immediate. The symptoms are dizziness, slurred speech, difficulty in swallowing, blurred vision, laboured breathing and unconsciousness. In the case of a Black Mamba bite, death can occur in anything from about 20 minutes to eight hours. Curiously, the major cause of death is not always respiratory failure, but paralysis of the swallowing mechanism, which can cause the patient to drown in his own saliva.

The coffin-shaped head of the Black Mamba

COBRAS Genus Naja (Neurotoxic venom)

Body shape: All members of this genus are capable of spreading a 'hood' which may equal three times the width of the body. The hood is only spread when they are threatened. Like Mambas, they are long, slender snakes, but they can be distinguished from Mambas when they are not spreading their hoods by the short snout, which is broader than it is long. They range in length from 1,5m to about 3m. **Fangs:** The fangs are situated in bulbous sheaths between the eye and the snout and there are usually two pairs, one pair being functional and the other pair as a reserve. **Venom:** As with Mambas the venom is neurotoxic and the symptoms are the same. The exception is the venom of the Mozambique Spitting Cobra (*Naja mossambica*), which may also exhibit cytotoxic (cellular destructive) symptoms. The Mozambique Spitting Cobra also has the ability to squirt its venom, but this is only toxic if it gets into the eyes or into a scratch or wound. The Egyptian Cobra (*Naja haje*) and the Cape Cobra (*Naja nivea*), the latter which occurs only in southern Africa, are responsible for the majority of early deaths in the overall incidence of snakebites.

A typical hood of an Egytian Cobra

SAN PARKS

Black Mamba (*Dendroaspis polylepus*)

TREE SNAKE / BOOMSLANG
Genus Dispholidus (Haemotoxic venom)

Body shape: Although the Tree Snake/ Boomslang (*Dispholidus typus typus*) is usually green, it can be confused with the Black Mamba or the Olive Grass Snake when it occurs in an olive-brown phase. The Boomslang can be distinguished by its short, stubby head, its exceptionally large eyes and keeled dorsal scales. **Fangs:** It has large fangs situated in the back of the mouth. **Venom:** The venom is haemotoxic, which means it results in severe internal bleeding by preventing the blood from clotting. Symptoms are delayed, developing 24 to 48 hours after the bite. A specific anti-venom for Tree Snake/Boomslang bite is required and, if not available, blood plasma transfusions may be given to replace the clotting agents.

Tree Snake/Boomslang

VINE SNAKE: Genus Thelotornis
(Haemotoxic venom)

Body shape: The Vine Snake (*Thelotornis capensis capensis*) is also known as the Bird Snake or Twig Snake. It is a slender snake with a lance-shaped head which becomes markedly vertically inflated when threatened. It has a cryptic colouration consisting of white, brown and black blotches. It is believed to have keener vision than other snakes because of the eyes being set further forward, giving them binocular vision. They have a characteristic key-hole shaped pupil. **Fangs:** Like the Boomslang, it is a back-fanged snake. **Venom:** The Bird snake has a potent haemotoxic venom which is not neutralised by the Boomslang-specific anti-venom. Treatment at this stage, until an effective anti-venom is found, is done only by blood transfusions. Human fatalities are rare.

Vine Snake

AFRICAN ROCK PYTHON (*Python sebae*)
The African Rock Python is the largest snake in Africa, reaching up to 5,6m in length. The longest record claimed is 10m, a West African specimen. Pythons may reach an age of 25 years or more. The Python is not poisonous, but uses its power to constrict its prey and death usually results from asphyxiation. It has been known to swallow antelopes the size of Impalas. There are also known cases where humans have been killed and swallowed, but very few authenticated records exist. Pythons possess heat-sensitive labial pits, an adaptation which enables them to strike very accurately at warm-blooded prey in the dark. The vestigial femurs (thigh bones) can clearly be seen as small 'spurs', which feature highly in various cultural rituals as charms, medicine ingredients or indicators. The backbone of a Python is often used to treat back problems by burning it and rubbing the ashes into incisions on the back. Some traditional healers wear the backbone of a Python around their necks to help the divining spirits to enter them. Python fat is used as an ointment to bring respect and prestige. It is also used as a love potion and a cure for leprosy. Today the African Rock Python is a protected species in most countries in Africa and Python trade is illegal.

African Rock Python (Python sebae)

SAN PARKS

REPTILES AND AMPHIBIANS

Lizards differ from snakes in that they have moveable eyelids, external ears and the two halves of the lower jaw are fused. Many Lizards and Skinks can shed their tails and regrow new ones. The most common lizard-like reptiles we encounter in Africa are the Monitor Lizards, Lizards, Skinks, Geckos, Agama Lizards and the Chameleons.

Nile or Water Monitor (Varanus niloticus)

Nile or Water Monitor (Varanus niloticus)

Flap-necked Chameleon (Chamaeleo dilepis)

Flap-necked Chameleon (Chamaeleo dilepis)

Rock Agama (Agama agama)

Common Flat Lizard (Platysaurus intermedius)

Gecko (Pachydactylus sp.)

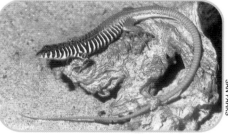

Striped Sandveld Lizard (Nucras tessellata)

Tortoises & Terrapins

The first tortoises date back about 210 million years. The Tortoise has both a skeleton and a protective, horny shell. The horny shell is attached to a bony case which in turn is fused to the rib cage. The peculiar result is that the shoulder blades and hip bones are situated within the rib cage. They all lay eggs and incubation can take anything from 4 to 15 months. There is a distinction between tortoises and terrapins. Tortoises are terrestrial and terrapins are semi-aquatic in fresh water. Turtles are found only in the ocean.

Tortoises eat mainly grass and forbs (small herbs) whereas terrapins are carnivorous. Terrapins submerge themselves at the water's edge and catch birds up to the size of doves, as they come down to drink.

Parrot-beaked Tortoise (Homopus areolatus)

Leopard Tortoise (Geochelone pardalis)

Angulate Tortoise (Chersina angulata)

Tent Tortoise (Pysammobates tentorius)

Hinged Tortoise (Kinikye sp.)

Serrated Terrapin (Pelusios subniger)

INTERESTING FACTS ABOUT AMPHIBIANS

Like reptiles, amphibians are ectothermic vertebrates, which means that they depend on outside heat sources rather than metabolic heat. In general, they are referred to as cold-blooded, but that is a confusing term as their blood is not cold.

Feeding Frogs and toads are carnivorous, feeding mainly on insects. They have large gapes and their tongues are essential feeding tools as they are sticky and used to transfer food to the mouth. The teeth are reduced or absent in some genera, as they mainly use them to restrain prey. The bullfrog has large projections on the lower jaw which serve the function of teeth.

Calls Only adult males produce calls during the breeding season, as they attract females that are ready to mate by means of sound, not vision or smell. Calling often intensifies after heavy rainstorms. There are always more males ready to mate than females. A female usually only mates once or twice in a season while males mate repeatedly.

Sound is produced by inflating the lungs and shifting the air from the lungs to the buccal cavity, causing the vocal cords of the larynx to vibrate. The sound is intensified by resonance in a thin-walled extension of the buccal cavity - the vocal sack. The air is shunted back and forth to produce repeated calls.

Mating The female advertises her availability by approaching the male closely, after which clasping will ensue. The correct term for clasping is 'amplexus'. Fertilisation is external and therefore the male does not have a sexual organ to insert spermatozoa into the female. There are three kinds of clasping - under the forearms, clasping around the waist and an unusual kind employed by rainfrogs, where the male adheres to the female, literally because the arms are to short to clasp.

Amplexus usually only lasts about 30 minutes but may last a few weeks in some species. After clasping, the male prods the flanks of the female with his forearms. The male is always smaller than the female, causing the two cloacae to be very close during egg-laying. As the eggs are ejected the ejaculation of siminal fluid by the male follows. The sequence is repeated several times. Some toads may lay up to 20 000 eggs but the rain frogs only lay 25 to 50 eggs.

The eggs The eggs are only about 1mm to 2mm in diameter. In the female's body they are covered by a jelly-like secretion. This causes the eggs to form clusters or strings. Tree Frogs 'whip up' the eggs into a stiff foam which is suspended on branches over water - a familiar sight in the bush. The foam forms a hard protective crust to prevent dehydration of the eggs. As the tadpoles are ready to hatch, they become heavy and the foam nest breaks open into the water.

Metamorphosis

Amphibian development involves metamorphosis in which the larva takes on a fish-like shape called a tadpole. In puddle-breeding species the larval or tadpole life may be just a few short weeks but with species that breed in permanent water it may be as long as nine months or even more. The tadpole stage of Rain Frogs, which burrow, take place underground within a jelly encasement. Metamorphosis involves both physical and physiological changes. They loose their tails, gills, larval mouth and develop a tympanum, eyelids, tongue and a cornified skin. They change from ammonia excretion to urea excretion and from being herbivorous to being carnivorous.

Metamorphosis (tadpole to frog/toad)

DIFFERENCES BETWEEN TOADS, FROGS AND CLAWLESS FROGS

Frogs and toads belong to the order Anura which can be further divided into those with tongues (frogs and toads) and those without tongues (*Aglossa*) to which the well-known Clawless Frog (*Xenopus laevis*) belongs.

Difference between frogs and toads: The main difference between toads and frogs is that toads are more land-bound and frogs are more water-bound. They both belong to the suborder *Neobatrachia* which consists of three superfamilies namely *Bufonoidea*, *Microhyloidea* and *Ranoidea*.

Toads (Superfamily *Bufonoidea*): Their skins are typically covered in rough, wart-like skin glands. The skin appears drier and they are more terrestrial, therefore well-adapted to drier climates. Other characteristics of toads include parotid glands in the ear region, a horizontal pupil and fingers that lack webbing. They spend most of their lives on dry land. They secrete a milky white toxin to deter predators. The most common representative is the Common Toad (*Bufo gutturalis*).

A typical toad

Rain Frogs and Banded Rubber Frogs (Superfamily *Microhyloidea*): The bold colouring of the **Banded Rubber Frog** suggests that it is poisonous and it is ignored by predators. The **Common Rain Frog** is particularly evident after the first rains in spring when it emerges from its burrow and utters a loud, eerie call, best described as a 'trilled, falsetto, yearning cry'. The eggs are laid in the burrow, each with a jelly encasement in which the tadpoles develop.

Other frogs (Superfamily *Ranoidea*): This family represents all the other frogs. **Bullfrog:** The Bullfrog (*Pyxicephalus adspersus adspersus*) is the largest frog in Africa, reaching ±21cm in length. The tadpoles are up to 7cm long. The call can be compared to the lowing of cattle repeated at short intervals.

A Typical Frog

These frogs are eagerly eaten by predators and humans. **Foamnest Tree Frog:** The cricket-ball sized nests of the grey-coloured Foamnest Tree Frog (*Chiromantis xerampelina*) is a familiar sight during the rainy season. **Reed Frogs:** The most commonly seen representatives are the Painted Reed Frog (*Hyperolius marmoratus*) and the Waterlily Frog (*Hyperolius pusillus*).

Clawless Frog: It differs from toads and frogs in that it has no tongue, no ears and it also has no eyelids. The front legs are small and flat with thin fingers and no claws - hence the common name. The female Clawless Frog was extensively used in the past for pregnancy tests. About 2,5cc chemically treated urine of an expectant woman was injected into the frog and if the test was positive, the frog would lay several thousand eggs within six or twelve hours. If negative, there would be no eggs. These frogs were exported to America in their thousands and very nearly became extinct. Fortunately a chemical pregnancy test was discovered in 1966 and saved them from their doom. With this dicovery there were thousands of surplus Clawless Frogs that were thrown out and they have subsequently become a pest, especially in California where they have taken over lakes and streams, impacting negatively on aquatic fauna.

Rain Frog (Breviceps sp.)

Clawless Frog (Xenopus laevis)

REPTILES AND AMPHIBIANS

REPTILES AND AMPHIBIANS

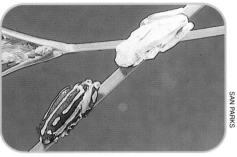
Bullfrog (Pyxicephalus adspersus)

Painted Reed Frog (Hyperolius marmoratus)

Banded Rubber Frog (Phrynomantis bifasciatus)

Clawless Frog (Xenopus laevis)

Toad (Bufo sp.)

Rain Frog (Breviceps sp.)

Snoring Puddle Frog (Phrynobatrachus natalensis)

River Frog (Rana sp.)

BIRDS

Greater Flamingo

Birds of prey

Birds of prey Birds of prey have exceptional eyesight, keener than all animals and far superior to humans. All birds of prey have comparatively large eyes with a high concentration of nerve cells and very highly developed eye muscles. In the light-sensitive retina, which is the central area of the eye, there is a depression known as the foveal pit containing light-sensitive cones or cells. A Buzzard, for example, has about one million of these cones per mm^2, as opposed to only about 125 000 in man. This suggests that they can see eight times better than humans. The fact that they can spot a rodent from such vast distances is because they have built-in telescopic vision. As the light rays strike the pit, they are bent outwards, thus magnifying the image by as much as 30%. Predatory birds always approach their prey at high speed and therefore need to gauge the distance and adjust their focus. Hawks have two fovea in each eye, one directed forwards and the other to the side to aid them in gauging distance. Falcons often catch their prey in the air at speeds of up to 200kph. To enable them to keep their prey in sharp focus, their eye muscles are extremely well developed. This helps to control the curvature of the lens and thus adjust the focal length.

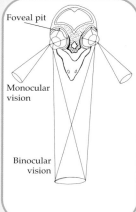

Foveal pit

Monocular vision

Binocular vision

Birds of prey have two foveal pits in each eye

Head of Buzzard

Lions have forward looking eyes, which gives them binocular vision

Other animals Antelopes have a horizontal pupil, enabling them to see more or less behind them from the outside corner of the eye. This is aided by the fact that the eyes are situated on the sides of the head, influencing their binocular vision - in other words, they cannot judge distances very well. Animals that need an acute depth perception in order to hunt or to climb trees and jump from branch to branch therefore have forward-looking eyes. The best examples are cats and primates. In this regard, the Klipspringer differs from other antelopes in that the eyes are set further forward in the skull in order to enable it to judge distances when jumping from rock to rock. People often wonder why the eyes of mammals, excluding humans, glow at night when a light is shone on them. The light is bounced back through the sensitive cells of the retina, by reflective crystals at the back of the eyes, called the tapetum. The presence of these crystals increases the chance of triggering a nerve impulse because the light moves twice through the light-sensitive retina. This is why nocturnal mammals have such excellent eyesight. A Lion, for instance, can see in light only one sixth of the brightness of that required by humans, enabling it to hunt at night.

BIRDS

148

Ostiches

Origination   Fossil evidence shows that the Ostriche originated in Europe and gradually migrated about 10 000km south to Africa.

Size   A large male Ostrich can stand over 2,5m tall and weigh as much as 160kg, making it the largest living bird in the world.

Longevity   In captivity they can live up to 50 years.

Water requirements   Provided they feed on succulent vegetation and insects, Ostriches can survive without surface water for an extended period.

Habitat preference   They prefer arid areas.

Food preference   Ostriches have an extremely varied diet, but fresh green grass features high up on the list of favourites.   Their flattened beak is an ideal tool for plucking the leaves off the grass stems, for stripping the seeds or for tearing the whole grass out, root and all, which they swallow together with large amounts of soil.   They have been known to eat almost anything from pebbles to plastic, the pebbles being essential for the proper digestion of their food.   Studies done in the Sahara showed that, included in the ±27kg of assorted material in the gizzard of an adult male Ostrich, there was about 4,5kg of oval-shaped pebbles!

Thermoregulation   Birds do have an advantage over mammals in that their body temperature is on average 3°C higher at about 40°C.   Therefore, in temperatures below 40°C they actually loose heat to the environment.   When the ambient temperature rises above 40°C, they apply gular fluttering - the same as panting in mammals.   The Camel and the Ostrich are the only known vertebrates to exhale air that is not fully saturated with water vapour.   In the case of the Ostrich it can at times be only 87% saturated and up to 4°C cooler than the body temperature.   One of the negative effects of panting or gular fluttering is that the lungs can become over-ventilated, resulting in a decrease in the carbon dioxide (CO_2) pressure in the blood and an alkaline shift of the blood pH - a process known as alkalosis. It has been found that the Ostrich can withstand air temperatures of 50°C for as long as five hours while applying gular fluttering constantly, at 50 cycles per minute, without any alkalosis taking place (Schmidt - Nielsen, 1978). Ostriches enhance their physiological attributes to keep their body temperature down by creating their own shade with their wing feathers, especially on their exposed thighs. Simultaneously they expose the naked undersides of their wings to wind cooling, thus removing trapped heat.   They orientate their long axis towards the sun to get the minimum of direct radiation from the sun.

Predator defence mechanisms   Its defenses against predators are its keen eyesight, its lethal karate kick and its ability to out-run most predators over long distances.   Adults are said to keep up the speed of 60kph to 70kph for considerable distances and 80kph at a sprint.   This makes them the fastest creature on two legs.   Because of its weight, an Ostrich will have to run a great deal faster if it wanted to fly - an estimated 1 000kph!

Breeding   Ostriches have communal nests. Up to three females will lay their eggs in one nest, and these will be incubated by the male and the dominant hen - also referred to as the alpha hen.   As laying takes place over at least two weeks, it is a mystery how they synchronise the hatching.

Ostriches

BIRDS

Birds of the Serengeti National Park

518 bird species have been recorded in the Serengeti National Park of which some are resident and some migratory. Because of the variety of habitat types, from dry bush to grassland to salt lakes, to riverine forest, the diversity of birds is spectacular. There are more bird species in the Serengeti Ecosystem than on the entire North American continent.

Many water birds are attracted by salt lakes and the variety and numbers at Lake Magadi near Moru kopjes and Lake Ndutu are very high. The Tawny Eagle, the Eastern Pale Chanting Goshawk and the Montagu's Harrier are the most common raptors on the open plains. They can often be seen along the roads. The Fischer's lovebird is endemic to northern Tanzania and the Yellow-collared Lovebird can also be seen there although it is rather rare. The commonly seen Rufous-tailed Weaver is another species that is endemic to northern Tanzania.

Summer (October to April) is the best time for bird-watching in the Serengeti as there are many European migrants during this time. Some of them breed in Africa but others escape the cold winters of the northern hemisphere. Bird-viewing at Lake Ndutu is particularly good during summer. Most of the vultures that occur in the Serengeti also nest there, except for the Reuppell's Griffon which nests mainly in the Olkarien Gorge in the Ngorongoro Conservation Area. Vultures are known to follow the migration and can do up to a 140km - a round trip of 280km - sometimes in one day! Flamingos mainly nest on Lake Natron and they travel very far to feed. In the Serengeti they can be seen at Lake Ndutu and Lake Magadi near Moru Kopjes. During summer the White Stork is one of the most common birds to be seen on the plains.

Quick alphabetical reference to the bird groups

Take note: The numbers refer to the numbers in the bird checklist:

Quick alphabetical reference to the bird groups

BIRDS

Bird check list

1   Ostrich

Ostrich

Ostrich ☐

An Ostrich egg contains the equivalent of two dozen hens' eggs. The male, with its black feathers, incubates at night and the grey-brown female during the day. An adult male stands over 2,5m tall and weighs about 160kg.

2   Pelicans

Great White Pelican

Pink-backed Pelican

Great White Pelican ☐

Pink-backed Pelican ☐

The Pelican has a dispensable pouch under its lower mandible which is used to scoop up fish. They form joint fishing parties, herding and cornering the fish. They cannot fly with fish in the pouch, as it will upset their centre of gravity. Fish for nestlings is swallowed and later regurgitated. The chick inserts its head into the adult's gullet to get its food. The White Pelican nests on the ground while the Pink-backed Pelican nests in trees. They do round trips of up to 200km per day for food.

3   Storks

Abdim's Stork

African Open-billed Stork

Abdim's Stork ☐
African Open-billed Stork ☐
Black Stork ☐
Marabou Stork ☐
Saddle-billed Stork ☐
White Stork ☐
Whoolly-necked Stork ☐
Yellow-billed Stork ☐

The Open-billed Stork has a gap between its mandibles to enable it to grasp the snails on which it feeds.

Marabou Stork   *Saddle-billed Stork*

Woolly Necked Stork   *Yellow-billed Stork*

The Saddle-billed Stork is the largest stork at 1,3m tall. The Marabou Stork has no feathers on its head and neck - an adaptation to feed on carrion, but it also eats fish, especially marooned Barbel.

4   Herons

Black-headed Heron

Green-backed Heron

Black-headed Heron ☐
Black Heron ☐
Green-backed Heron ☐
Madagascar Squacco Heron ☐
Scuacco Heron ☐
Black-crowned Night Heron ☐
Goliath Heron ☐
Grey Heron ☐
Purple Heron ☐
Rufous-bellied Heron ☐

Squacco Heron   *Grey Heron*

Bird check list

Black Heron

Purple Heron

Goliath Heron

Rufous-bellied Heron

5   Egrets

Great White Egret

Great White Egret ☐
Cattle Egret ☐
Yellow-billed Egret ☐
Little Egret ☐

The Great White Egret is the largest Egret with a distinct 'kink' in its neck, black legs and a yellow bill, which turns black during breeding. The Yellow-billed Egret always has a yellow bill, black legs with yellow thighs. The Little Egret has a black bill, black legs with yellow feet.

Cattle Egret

Yellow-billed Egret

Little Egret

6   Grebes / Dabchicks

Little Grebe / Dabchick

Little Grebe / Dabchick ☐
Black-necked Grebe ☐
Great Crested Grebe ☐

Dabchicks dive for frogs and tadpoles to eat.

Darters   7

African Darter

African Darter ☐

The African Darter uses its bill like a spear, diving at great speed and spearing its prey. They lack the protective oil layer on their feathers and thus need to dry their wings in the sun.

Cormorants   8

Long-tailed Cormorant

Great Cormorant ☐
Long-tailed Cormorant ☐

Cormorants dive under water to catch fish. The lack of oil on their feathers enables them to dive deeper but they cannot float like other water birds.

Bitterns   9

The Dwarf Bittern is an 'opportunistic breeder', favouring areas that are seasonally flooded.

Little Bittern ☐
Dwarf Bittern ☐

Hamerkops   10

Hamerkop

Hamerkop ☐

Hamerkops build huge nests of up to 1,5m in diameter that can weigh up to 50kg or more. Inside is a tunnel and chamber which are plastered with mud. They collect all kinds of objects such as plastic, metal and bones to decorate the nest.

Ibises   11

Sacred Ibis

Sacred Ibis ☐
Hadada Ibis ☐
Glossy Ibis ☐

The Hadada Ibis mates for life. They are grassland birds, foraging on the ground.

BIRDS

153

Bird check list

Hadada Ibis

Glossy Ibis

12 Flamingos

Greater Flamingo ☐

Lesser Flamingo ☐

Flamingos are filter feeders and feed almost exclusively on plankton - microscopic plants and animals that occur in mud and on the surface of shallow, saline lakes. The bill is sharply recurved and they invert their bill when feeding, using the tongue to pump the water through the filtering lamellae which allow only the plankton through. Lesser Flamingos select mainly for blue-green algae such as *Saliginella* and diatoms.

Greater Flamingo

Lesser Flamingo

13 Spoonbills

African Spoonbill ☐

Spoonbills feed by moving their slightly open, spatulate bill from side to side and taking in waterborne organisms, even small fish. They breed in Africa and roost communally, often on partially submerged trees.

African Spoonbill

14 Ducks

African Black Duck ☐

Fulvous Whistling Duck ☐

Knob-billed Duck ☐

Tufted Duck ☐

White-backed Duck ☐

Knob-billed Duck

There are no fish-eating ducks in Africa.

White-faced Whistling Duck ☐

Yellow-billed duck ☐

White-faced Whistling Duck

Yellow-billed Duck

Garganeys 15

Garganey ☐

Pintails 16

Northern Pintail ☐

Pochards 17

Southern Pochard ☐

Shoveller 18

Northern Shoveller ☐

Teals 19

Cape Teal ☐

Hottentot Teal ☐

Red-billed Teal ☐

The Red-billed Teal is a wanderer, covering distances of 1 600km per year.

Cape Teal

Hottentot Teal

Red-billed Teal

Wigeons 20

Eurasian Wigeon ☐

BIRDS

Bird check list

21 — Geese

African Pygmy Goose

- African Pygmy Goose ☐
- Egyptian Goose ☐
- Spur-winged Goose ☐

Although they are called Geese, there are no true geese in Africa south of the Sahara.

Egyptian Goose

Spur-winged Goose

22 — Jacanas

- African Jacana ☐

African Jacanas have a polyandrous mating system - that is where the females mate, lay the eggs and leave the male to raise the chicks. She may even destroy another male's eggs to get him to mate with her.

African Jacana

23 — Water Rails

- African Water Rail ☐

24 — Crakes

- Black Crake ☐
- African Crake ☐
- Corncrake ☐

The Black Crake feeds on small mollusks, crustaceans, insects, even small birds and eggs.

Black Crake

25 — Gallinules/Swamphens

- Purple Swamphen (Gallinule) ☐
- Allen's Gallinule ☐

26 — Moorhens

- Common Moorhen ☐
- Lesser Moorhen ☐

Moorhens feed on aquatic plants and animals and their nests consist of 'bowls' of reeds which they build in shallow water.

Common Moorhen

27 — Coots

Coots are monogamous.

- Red-knobbed Coot ☐

28 — Avocets

Avocets prefer pans in semi-arid areas.

- Eurasian Avocet ☐

29 — Stilts

- Common Stilt ☐

The Stilt has the longest legs in comparison with its body of any bird. Their nests are almost always surrounded by shallow water and consist of piled-up plant material. They frequently mob potential predators.

Common Stilt

30 — Thicknees

- Water Thicknee ☐
- Spotted Thicknee ☐

The large eyes of Thicknees indicate that they are semi-nocturnal, enabling them to see at night. The Water Thicknee is more diurnal. They both feed on insects, snails, frogs and crabs. The Water Thicknee even eats the shells of snails and crabs. Both have a characteristic whistle-like piping call, often heard at night. They both breed on the ground in shallow scrapes surrounded by pellets or animal droppings. The Water Thicknee usually nests closer to the water.

Water Thicknee

Spotted Thicknee

Bird check list

31 Gulls

Grey-headed Gull

Black-headed Gull ☐
Grey-headed Gull ☐
Lesser Black-backed Gull ☐

The Grey-headed Gull is a scavenger and will also kill nestlings of other water birds.

32 Terns

Whiskered Tern

Sandwich Tern ☐
Whiskered Tern ☐
White-winged Black Tern ☐

Terns feed by plucking from the surface or plunging into the water.

33 Skimmers

African Skimmer

African Skimmer ☐

The Skimmer feeds by flying close to the water with its bill open, the lower mandible scything the surface for fish. They nest in deep scrapes in the ground. They favour brackish lakes.

34 Coursers

Temminck's Courser

Temminck's Courser ☐
Two-banded Courser ☐
Violet-tipped Courser ☐
Three-banded/Heuglin's Courser ☐

Two-banded Courser   *Three-banded Courser*

Pratincoles 35

Commom Pratincole

Common Pratincole ☐

Pratincoles are monogamous and they nest on floodplain mudflats, almost always near water. They lay the eggs on bare ground, often in a hoofprint. A predator is lured away by the adult feigning injury.

Plovers 36

Kittlitz's Plover

Caspian Plover ☐
Little Ringed Plover ☐
Ringed Plover ☐
Kittlitz's Plover ☐
Three-banded Plover ☐
Chestnut-banded Plover ☐

Three-banded Plover   *Chestnut-banded Plover*

Lapwings 37

African Wattled Lapwing

African Wattled Lapwing ☐
Blacksmith Lapwing ☐
Black-winged Lapwing ☐
Crowned Lapwing ☐
Senegal Lapwing ☐
Spur-winged Lapwing ☐
Long-toed Lapwing ☐

Blacksmith Lapwing   *Crowned Lapwing*

Bird check list

Senegal Lapwing   *Long-toed Lapwing*

38 Curlews

Curlews are waders, having long, curved bills.

Eurasian Curlew ☐

39 Greenshanks

Greenshank ☐

The Greenshank is very similar to the Marsh Sandpiper, the Greenshank having a thicker, slightly upward curving bill and light green legs. They both wade in deeper water than other waders.

Greenshank

40 Godwits

Godwits have very long bills and the body shape of a Lapwing.

Black-tailed Godwit ☐

41 Redshanks

The legs and base of bill of a Redshank are red. They are waders, living on aquatic life.

Redshank ☐
Spotted Redshank ☐

42 Ruffs

Ruff ☐

Technically, the 'Ruff' is the male and the 'Reeve' is the female. Ruffs form large flocks. The male is much larger and their legs are orange. They breed in Europe and are summer migrants in Africa.

Ruff

Sandpipers 43

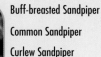

Buff-breasted Sandpiper ☐
Common Sandpiper ☐
Curlew Sandpiper ☐
Green Sandpiper ☐
Marsh Sandpiper ☐
Ruddy Sandpiper ☐
Terek Sandpiper ☐
Wood Sandpiper ☐

Common Sandpiper

Sandpipers often bob their heads whilst feeding - it is said to help with focusing on their underwater prey. They feed on small aquatic fauna.

Curlew Sandpiper

Marsh Sandpiper   *Wood Sandpiper*

Stints 44

Little Stint ☐
Temminck's Stint ☐

The Little Stint breeds in Europe and Asia and is a summer visitor in Africa. They usually forage in flocks. Their food is mollusks, crustaceans, insects and worms.

Little Stint

Snipes 45

African Snipe ☐
Common Snipe ☐
Great Snipe ☐
Painted Snipe ☐

The Common Snipe is a migrant.

Common Snipe

BIRDS

157

BIRDS

The Common Snipe has a very long bill which it uses to probe for aquatic fauna. The Painted Snipe has a polyandrous mating system, like the Jacana. The female may mate and produce eggs with up to four males in one season.

Painted Snipe

46 Cranes

Grey-crowned Crane ☐

Crowned Cranes roost in flocks of 10-200, often on islands within rivers. They feed solitary or in pairs. They feed on insects, frogs, reptiles and grain, even grass seeds which they strip off the standing grass.

Grey-crowned Crane

47 Secretary Bird

Secretary Bird ☐

The Secretary Bird feeds mainly on snakes, frogs, lizards and rodents. They swallow their prey whole. They are so named because of the quills on their head, reminiscent of a secretary with a pen above his/her ear.

Secretary Bird

48 Eagles

African Fish Eagle ☐
African Hawk Eagle ☐
Ayres's Hawk Eagle ☐
Bateleur Eagle ☐
Booted Eagle ☐
Brown Snake Eagle ☐
Crowned Eagle ☐
Imperial Eagle ☐
Lesser-spotted Eagle ☐
Long-crested Eagle ☐

African Fish Eagle

African Hawk Eagle

Martial Eagle ☐
Short-toed Snake Eagle ☐
Tawny Eagle ☐
Verreaux's Eagle ☐
Wahlberg's Eagle ☐

Bateleur Eagle

Bateleur Eagle (immature)   *Black-breasted Snake Eagle*

Brown Snake Eagle   *Martial Eagle*

Tawny Eagle (light)   *Tawny Eagle (dark)*

The eyes of birds of prey are positioned to the front of the head to provide them with binocular vision. All birds have colour vision. The vision of raptors is extremely good but their sense of smell is poor.

Verreaux's Eagle

Osprey 49

Osprey ☐

Ospreys feed on fish, plunging into the water feet first, sometimes submerging completely. They carry the fish by the head to offer the least wind resistance and their feet are rough to ensure a tight grip.

Osprey

Bird check list

50   Vultures

African White-backed Vulture ☐

Egyptian Vulture ☐

Hooded Vulture ☐

Lammergeier ☐

Lappet-faced Vulture ☐

Palm-nut Vulture ☐

Rueppell's Griffon ☐

White-headed Vulture ☐

African White-backed Vulture

Vultures feed on carrion. They have no feathers on their neck, enabling them to feed inside a carcass. Refer to pg 49 for more details.

Hooded Vulture

Lammergeier

Lappet-faced Vulture

Rueppell's Griffon

White-headed Vulture

51   Harriers

African Marsh Harrier ☐

Eurasian Marsh Harrier ☐

Montagu's Harrier ☐

Pallid Harrier ☐

Montagu's Harriers are very common on the Serengeti Plains.

Montagu's Harrier

African Marsh Harriers are associated with marshy areas, particularly reedbeds. They fly with their heads looking down whilst hunting. The male brings its prey to the female. She flies off the nest and takes it in full flight by a swift upside-down manoeuvre. They feed on frogs, rodents and birds.

African Marsh Harrier

Goshawks   52

African Goshawk ☐

Black Goshawk ☐

Eastern Pale Chanting ☐

Dark Chanting Goshawk ☐

Eastern Goshawk ☐

Gabar Goshawk ☐

Eastern Pale Chanting Goshawk (male)

Eastern Pale Chanting Goshawk (female)

Dark Chanting Goshawk

Gabar Goshawk

Gabar Goshawk (melanistic)

Goshawks are called 'short-winged hawks' (as opposed to the long-winged falcons). The Goshawk hunts in wooded country, watching from a perch and making a quick dash. A Gabar Goshawk's nest can be recognised by the spider web that forms part of it. The birds have been observed carrying Communal Spiders (*Stegodyphus sp.*) to their nest early in the nest-building process. Various suggestions have been put forward, such as camouflage, strengthening and parasite control, possibly a combination of all three.

BIRDS

BIRDS

53 Buzzards

Augur Buzzard ☐
Common Buzzard ☐
Grasshopper Buzzard ☐
Lizzard Buzzard ☐
Mountain Buzzard ☐
Western Honey-buzzard ☐

Augur Buzzard

Augur Buzzard (melanistic)

The Augur Buzzard frequents mountains and kopjes and they often nest on rock ledges. The nest is about 40cm across and they line the nest with the lichen, Old Man's Beard (*Usnea sp.*), where available. They eat mainly snakes, lizards, insects and birds.

54 Kestrels

Common Kestrel ☐
Grey-eyed Kestrel ☐
Lesser Kestrel ☐
White-eyed Kestrel ☐

Common Kestrel

Lesser Kestrel

The Lesser Kestrel is a palaearctic migrant, that means they breed in Europe but come to Africa during the European winter. The Greater Kestrel breeds in Africa and uses deserted nests of raptors, varying in size from a Secretary Bird to a Black-shouldered Kite, preferring that of Pied Crows. Kestrels eat mainly insects but also small rodents and birds.

55 Falcons

African Pygmy Falcon ☐
Eastern Red-footed Falcon ☐
Lanner Falcon ☐
Peregrine Falcon ☐
Red-necked Falcon ☐

Lanner Falcon

Lanner Falcon (juvenile)

Falcons strike at great speed and force from above, often killing their prey on impact. In East Africa, Pygmy Falcons nest in a chamber of the communal nests of White-headed Buffalo Weavers. A falcon's nest can be recognised by the ring of white droppings at the entrance.

Hawks 56

Hawks are short-winged and falcons long-winged. The Bat Hawk emerges at dusk and preys on bats, swifts and other late-flying birds. It swallows its prey whole in flight.

African Cuckoo-hawk ☐
African Harrier-hawk ☐
African Little Sparrow-hawk ☐
Bat Hawk ☐
Ovambo Sparrow-hawk ☐

Shikras 57

A Shikra is a hawk with red eyes.

Shikra ☐

Hobbies 58

Hobbies are actually just falcons, belonging to the same genus '*Falco*'.

African Hobbie ☐
Northern Hobbie ☐

Kites 59

Black Kite ☐
Black-shouldered Kite ☐

Black Kite

Black-shouldered Kite

The Black Kite can be recognised by its forked tail. It mainly scavenges, often ocurring at picnic sites. The Black-shouldered Kite is nomadic and roosts communally. Individuals are highly territorial. A female chooses the male with the best territory but she does not form a permanent bond with him. They do not have a distinct breeding season. It has been suggested that reproductive steroids in their rodent prey may trigger hormonal activity. They may raise a number of broods in one season.

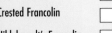

60 Francolins

Coqui Francolin ☐

Crested Francolin ☐

Hildebrandt's Francolin ☐

Shelley's Francolin ☐

Coqui Francolin

Francolins have highly developed gizzards consisting of a corrugated, leathery lining surrounded by muscular walls that contract rhythmically whilst strong enzymes are secreted to aid breakdown of the grain they swallow whole. They occur in family groups and feed on seeds, berries, insects and other invertebrates.

Crested Francolin

61 Spurfowl

Grey-breasted Spurfowl ☐

Red-necked Spurfowl ☐

Yellow-fronted Spurfowl ☐

The Yellow-fronted Spurfowl and the Grey-breasted Spurfowl often interbreed in the Serengeti area.

Yellow-fronted Spurfowl

62 Guineafowl

Helmeted Guineafowl ☐

Guineafowls are monogamous. They form flocks during the non-breeding season, forming pairs in early summer to breed solitary. They often nest within a few hundred metres of each other.

Helmeted Guineafowl

63 Quails

Blue Quail ☐

Common Quail ☐

Quails are rainy season migrants. The Common Quail prefers grassland and fallow lands but the Blue Quail prefers margins of seasonally waterlogged areas.

Common Quail

Bustards 64

Black-bellied Bustard ☐

Buff-crested Bustard ☐

Denham's Bustard ☐

Hartlaub's Bustard ☐

Kori Bustard ☐

White-bellied Bustard ☐

Black-bellied Bustard

Bustards are ground birds and they nest on the ground. They are well camouflaged but the males have very visual mating displays, inflating their gular pouches and puffing out their neck feathers. This may attract several females. The males will mate with more than one female and that is where their duty ends. They do not help with raising the chicks. The Kori Bustard is the heaviest flying bird in Africa.

White-bellied Bustard

Kori Bustard

Sandgrouse 65

Black-faced Sandgrouse ☐

Chestnut-bellied Sandgrouse ☐

Yellow-throated Sandgrouse ☐

Sandgrouse occur in arid environments.

Yellow-throated Sandgrouse

Pigeons 66

African Green Pigeon ☐

Olive Pigeon ☐

Speckled Pigeon ☐

African Green Pigeon

Nestlings are fed on 'pigeon's milk', very similar in substance to milk produced by mammals.

Speckled Pigeon

Bird check list

67 Doves

African Mourning Dove

African Mourning Dove ☐

Dusky Turtle Dove ☐

Emerald-spotted Wood Dove ☐

Laughing Dove ☐

Doves feed mainly on seeds, occasionally insects.

Dusky Turtle Dove

Emerald-spotted Wood Dove

Laughing Dove

Ring-necked Dove

68 Lovebirds

Fischer's Lovebird

Fischer's Lovebird ☐

Yellow-collared Lovebird ☐

The Fischers Lovebird is endemic to northern Tanzania. Their numbers have been depleted because of the overseas bird trade.

69 Parrots

Brown Parrot

African Orange-bellied Parrot ☐

Brown Parrot ☐

Red-fronted Parrot ☐

Parrots eat mainly fruit.

Go-away Birds 70

Bare-faced Go-away Bird

Bare-faced Go-away Bird ☐

White-bellied Go-away Bird ☐

Go-away Birds have a characteristic 'kwe' sounding call. Hunters believe they warn game to 'go away', hence the name 'Go-away Bird'. They have strong, curved bills which enable them to cope with tough fruit husks. They depend on the fruit of indigenous trees but do feed insects to their young. They are very agile in trees, moving with a light, springy action. They have a semi-zygodactylous toe formation in which the outer toe protrudes at right angles to the foot and is free to move backward or forward.

White-bellied Go-away Bird

Turacos 71

Turacos are colourful forest birds. Parents feed the chicks by regurgitating undigested berries. The chicks do not pass faecal sacs and therefore the adult pecks at the anus and eats the liquid excreta.

Green Turaco ☐

Puple-crested Turaco ☐

Ross's Turaco ☐

Cuckoos 72

Great Spotted Cuckoo

African Cuckoo ☐

African Emerald Cuckoo ☐

Black-and-white Cuckoo ☐

Black Cuckoo ☐

Diederik's Cuckoo ☐

Eurasian Cuckoo ☐

Great Spotted Cuckoo ☐

Klaas's Cuckoo ☐

Lesser Cuckoo ☐

Levaillant's Cuckoo ☐

Red-chested Cuckoo ☐

Great Spotted Cuckoo

73 — Coucals

Black Coucal ☐

White-browed Coucal ☐

Black Coucal

Coucals are also called 'Bottle Birds' because their call resembles water bubbling out of a bottle. They are closely related to cuckoos but do not display parasitic behaviour. Most species are monogamous, except for the Black Coucal which can also be polyandrous (where a female mates and raises chicks with more than one male). Their eyes only open after ±5 days. They defend themselves by hissing like a snake and by voiding nauseating liquid faeces (different to the encapsulated faecal sack that they normally produce).

White-browed Coucal

74 — Mousebirds

Blue-naped Mousebird ☐

Speckled Mousebird ☐

Speckled Mousebird

Mousebirds have the ability to turn their outer toes forwards or backwards, enabling them to creep along branches like mice. They often hang upside down and are even known to sleep like that.

75 — Owls

African Marsh Owl

African Wood Owl

African Grass Owl ☐

African Marsh Owl ☐

African Wood Owl ☐

Barn Owl ☐

Common Scops Owl ☐

White-faced Scops Owl ☐

Pearl-spotted Owlet ☐

Spotted Eagle-owl ☐

Verreaux's Eagle-owl ☐

Owls can turn their heads through 270° and have superior night vision.

Barn Owl

Common Scops Owl

White-faced Scops Owl

Pearl-spotted Owlet

Spotted Eagle-owl

Verreaux's Eagle-owl

Nightjars — 76

Dusky Nightjar ☐

Eurasian Nightjar ☐

Gabon Nightjar ☐

Slender-tailed Nightjar ☐

Pennant-wing Nighjar ☐

Nightjar

Swifts — 77

Swifts feed, mate and collect nesting material on the wing. The European Swift remains airborne for 9 months of the year, only using a nest during breeding. It even sleeps in the air by ascending to great heights where its metabolism drops and it goes into a state of semi-sleep.

African Black Swift ☐

African Palm Swift ☐

Eurasian Swift ☐

Little Swift ☐

Mottled Swift ☐

Nyanza Swift ☐

Scarce Swift ☐

Bird check list

78 Spinetails

They are often associated with Baobab Trees. Their nests are vertical on branches.

Mottled Spinetail ☐

79 Kingfishers

African Pygmy Kingfisher ☐
Brown-hooded Kingfisher ☐
Giant Kingfisher ☐
Grey-headed Kingfisher ☐
Half-collared Kingfisher ☐
Malachite Kingfisher ☐
Pied Kingfisher ☐
Striped Kingfisher ☐
Woodland Kingfisher ☐

Not all Kingfishers eat fish, some eat insects.

Brown-hooded Kingfisher

Giant Kingfisher

Grey-headed Kingfisher

Half-collared Kingfisher

Malachite Kingfisher

Pied Kingfisher

Striped Kingfisher

Woodland Kingfisher

Trogons 80

Trogons are bright in colour and prefer riverine forest and dense woodland .

Bar-tailed Trogon ☐
Nerina's Trogon ☐

Bee-eaters 81

Blue-cheeked Bee-eater ☐
Cinnamon-chested Bee-eater ☐
Eurasian Bee-eater ☐
Little Bee-eater ☐
Olive Bee-eater ☐
Swallow-tailed Bee-eater ☐
White-throated Bee-eater ☐

Bee-eaters use their long, curved bills to dig their nesting tunnels in earth embankment, using their feet as shovels.

Blue-cheecked Bee-eater

Eurasian Bee-eater

Swallow-tailed Bee-eater

White-throated Bee-eater

Rollers 82

Broad-billed Roller ☐
Eurasian Roller ☐
Lilac-breasted Roller ☐
Rufous-crowned Roller ☐

'Roller' refers to their flight display.

Broad-billed Roller

Lilac-breasted Roller

Eurasian Roller

83   Hoopoes

African Hoopoe ☐

Green Wood Hoopoe ☐

African Hoopoe

The African Hoopoe utters a melodious hoop-hoop call but Green Wood Hoopoes travel in groups and are very noisy, sounding like a group of women laughing, as many of their African names indicate. The African Hoopoe often has two or three broods in the same season. It is referred to in the Old Testament as regards its poor nest sanitation. Their long bills enable them to probe under bark and in grass roots for invertebrates.

Green Wood Hoopoe

84   Scimitarbills

Scimitarbills are Wood Hoopoes have prominently curved bills.

Abyssinian Scimitarbill ☐

Scimitarbill ☐

85   Hornbills

African Grey Hornbill

African Grey Hornbill ☐

Black-and-white Casqued Hornbill ☐

Crowned Hornbill ☐

Red-billed Hornbill ☐

Silvery-cheeked Hornbill ☐

Southern Ground Hornbill ☐

Trumpeter Hornbill ☐

Von der Decken's Hornbill ☐

Red-billed Hornbill

Southern Ground Hornbill

Trumpeter Hornbill

Von der Decken's Hornbill

Hornbills have horn-shaped, curved bills and feed on fruit, berries and some species of insects. They feed by taking the food in the tip of the bill, toss it into the air and swallow it. They drink in the same way, dipping the bill in water, tossing and catching an individual drop in the mouth.

Tinkerbirds   86

Tinkerbirds are also known as tinker-barbets. They are large-headed with a stout bill and are usually strongly marked. Their wings are short and rounded, producing noisy flight.

Moustached Green Tinkerbird ☐

Red-fronted Tinkerbird ☐

Yellow-rumped Tinkerbird ☐

Barbets   87

Crested Barbet

Black-billed Barbet ☐

Black-throated Barbet ☐

Crested Barbet ☐

D'Arnaud's Barbet ☐

Double-toothed Barbet ☐

Red-and-yellow Barbet ☐

Red-fronted Barbet ☐

Spotted-flanked Barbet ☐

Usimbiro Barbet ☐

White-headed Barbet ☐

D'Arnaud's Barbet

Woodpeckers   88

Bearded Woodpecker

Bearded Woodpecker ☐

Bennet's Woodpecker ☐

Brown-backed Woodpecker ☐

Cardinal Woodpecker ☐

Golden-tailed Woodpecker ☐

Green-backed Woodpecker ☐

BIRDS

Bird check list

BIRDS

Grey Woodpecker ☐

Nubian Woodpecker ☐

Woodpeckers have extremely long and mobile tongues which they use to probe under the bark of trees. They have thick skulls and powerful neck muscles to withstand the hammering.

Cardinal Woodpecker

Golden-tailed Woodpecker

Nubian Woodpecker

89 — Broadbills

It is a thickset, arboreal forest bird with a large head and broad, flat bill.

African Broadbill ☐

90 — Honeyguides

Honeyguides are the only known birds able to digest bees wax. They guide humans or honey badgers to a nest by flight display and chirring noises. Their skins are extra tough to withstand stings.

Greater Honeyguide ☐

Lesser Honeyguide ☐

Scaly-throated Honeyguide ☐

Wahlberg's Honeyguide ☐

91 — Larks

African Short-toed Lark (Red-capped Lark)

Crested Lark

African Short-toed Lark/Red-capped Lark ☐

African Singing Bushlark ☐

Crested Lark ☐

Fawn-coloured Lark ☐

Flappet Lark ☐

Short-tailed Lark ☐

Somali Short-toed Lark ☐

Rufous-naped Lark ☐

White-tailed Bushlark ☐

Rufous-naped Lark

African Larks all have beautiful songs. The African species are terrestrial with plainly-coloured plumage. The back is scaled and not plain like the pipits. All species nest on the ground but they do perch on trees and posts as well. Their diet is largely insects but some feed on seeds also.

Sparrow-larks — 92

Chestnut-backed Sparrow-lark

Chestnut-backed Sparrow-lark ☐

Fischer's Sparrow-lark ☐

Sparrow-larks or Finch-larks are small birds that breed in semi-arid habitats with sparse ground cover. They nest in an open cup in a scrape in the ground.

Pipits — 93

Richard's Pipit

Bush Pipit ☐

Long-billed Pipit ☐

Red-throated Pipit ☐

Richard's Pipit ☐

Tree Pipit ☐

Swallows — 94

Rufous-breasted Swallow

Wire-tailed Swallow

Angola Swallow ☐

Barn Swallow ☐

Grey-rumped Swallow ☐

Mosque Swallow ☐

Lesser-striped Swallow ☐

Red-rumped Swallow ☐

Rufous-breasted Swallow ☐

White-tailed Swallow ☐

Wire-tailed Swallow ☐

Swallows have broad bills with wide gapes used as insect traps.

Bird check list

95   Martins

Martins are perching birds that have developed an aerial way of feeding. Their legs are short and weak but their wing-muscles are superior.

- Brown-throated Sand-martin ☐
- Common Sand-martin ☐
- Rock Martin ☐
- Western House Martin ☐

96   Saw-wings

Saw-wings are actually swallows and feed on insects whilst in flight.

- Black Saw-wing ☐
- White-headed Saw-wing ☐

97   Longclaws

Rosy-breasted Longclaw

Yellow-throated Lonclaw

- Pangani Longclaw ☐
- Rosy-breasted Longclaw ☐
- Yellow-throated Longclaw ☐

Longclaws are grassland birds of water-logged areas, spending much time on the ground. Their feet are stout and the hind claw is very long. They are related to wagtails and pipits. They often mount grass tussocks to look around. Their nests are neatly lined cups, often at the base of a grass tuft and are well concealed. The tail of the Rosy-breasted Longclaw is longer than that of other longclaws.

98   Wagtails

African Pied Wagtail

Yellow Wagtail

- African Pied Wagtail ☐
- Grey Wagtail ☐
- Mountain Wagtail ☐
- Yellow Wagtail ☐

Wagtails are monogamous and probably pair for life. They are aggressively territorial. Both build the nest and the male offers nest-building material to the female any time of the year to maintain the bond. Both tend to the chicks. The Pied Wagtail breeds in Africa but the Yellow Wagtail is a palaearctic migrant.

Cuckooshrikes   99

Cuckooshrikes are related to drongos and have no affinities with either shrikes or cuckoos. They have a slight terminal hook on the rather small bill.

- Black Cuckooshrike ☐
- Grey-throated Cuckooshrike ☐
- Purple-throated Cuckooshrike ☐

Bulbuls   100

Common Bulbul

Yellow-bellied Bulbul

- Common Bulbul ☐
- Yellow-bellied Bulbul ☐

Except for the Common Bulbul, which is quite bold, others in this group, like the greenbuls, are rather secretive. The Yellow-bellied Bulbul is confined to thick undergrowth in forests and is very shy. The Common Bulbul occurs almost everywhere except above 3 000m. Plumage is soft with long lower back feathers and hair-like feathers on the nape. They feed on fruit, insects and nectar. The nest is a flimsy cup. Parental care by both sexes.

Greenbuls   101

Greenbuls are very shy birds.

- Olive Mountain Greenbul ☐

Wheatears   102

Capped Wheatear

- Capped Wheatear ☐
- Isabeline Wheatear ☐
- Mourning Wheatear ☐
- Northern Wheatear ☐
- Pied Wheatear ☐

Thrushes   103

Kurrichane Thrush

- Bare-eyed Thrush ☐
- Common Rock-thrush ☐
- Kurrichane Thrush ☐
- Olive Thrush ☐
- Spotted Morning-thrush ☐

BIRDS

Bird check list

Olive Thrush

Thrushes are ground birds, occuring solitary or in pairs. They run for a few paces, stop, turn their heads and literally listen for insect movement below the soil surface. They feed on insects, mollusks, spiders and lizards. They nest in tree-forks and nests are lined with mud.

Heuglin's Robin-chat

Robin-chats are monogamous, territorial and they pair for life. They maintain their territory throughout the year. The Cape and Heuglin's Robin-chats are both parasitised by the Red-chested Cuckoo. They have both adapted well to gardens.

104 Chats

Common Stonechat

- Alpine Chat ☐
- Common Stonechat ☐
- Familiar Chat ☐
- Irania (Chat) ☐
- Mocking Cliff Chat ☐
- Northern Ant-eating Chat ☐
- Whinchat ☐

Mocking Cliff Chat

Chats do not migrate, some make minor movements. All are monogamous and territorial. Chat males show off white patches in their plumage to attract females. Most chats have their nests on the ground under a rock. They build a base of stones, earth, bark, with a small cup for the actual nest. The Ant-eating Chat nests in the walls of Aardvark, Porcupine and Hyena dens and the tunnel to the nest is just under one metre long. The nest itself is also cup-shaped.

Northern Ant-eating Chat

105 Robins

The bills of robins are slender for picking up insects.

- White-browed Scrub-robin ☐
- White-starred Robin ☐

106 Robin-chats

The Cape Robin-chat can be distinguished from the Heuglin's Robin-chat by a shorter white eyebrow and by the greyish-white underparts. They occur in forest edges and are common garden visitors.

- Cape Robin-chat ☐
- White-browed Robin-chat ☐
- Heuglin's Robin-chat ☐
- Red-capped Robin-chat ☐
- Rueppell's Robin-chat ☐

107 Blackcaps

The Blackcap is a Warbler with a black cap.

- Blackcap (Warbler) ☐

108 Camaropteras

The Common Camaroptera is also known as the Grey-backed Bleating Warbler.

- Common Camaroptera (Warbler) ☐

109 Warblers

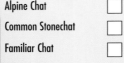

Grey-backed Bleating Warbler

- African Reed Warbler ☐
- Brown Warbler ☐
- Buff-bellied Warbler ☐
- Eurasian Reed Warbler ☐
- Garden Warbler ☐
- Great Reed Warbler ☐
- Grey-backed Bleating Warbler ☐
- Grey Bush-warbler ☐
- Icterine Warbler ☐
- Lesser Swamp Warbler ☐
- Miomobo Bush-warbler ☐
- Olivaceous Warbler ☐
- Olive Tree Warbler ☐
- Red-faced Warbler ☐
- Sedge Warbler ☐
- Willow Warbler ☐

Warblers are extremely vocal, skulking and elusive with small slender bills to eat insects. They are mostly identified by their calls which they use to advertise their territories, maintaining the pair bond for courtship. The Bleating Warbler is unmistakable by its bleat-like call, it also emits a repeated chitip-chitip and produces a trip sound with its wings. Nests consist of growing leaves sewn together with spider web, by pinching holes in the leaves and threading them together with short lengths of spider web.

110 Whitethroats

- Common Whitethroat ☐

BIRDS

168

Bird check list

Cisticolas   111

Cisticolas can be described as grass warblers because of their preference for grassy habitats in open veld and near streams. They are russet on top, streaked with black and characteristically pale to cream below. They are small birds and the tail is often cocked up. They are mostly seen hanging on grass stems looking for insects. They construct bottle-shaped nests. Cisticolas are known as the most frustrating 'little brown jobs' because they all look similar and have three different plumages - juvenile, breeding and non-breeding. Their name refers to the sound they make.

- Ashy Cisticola ☐
- Croaking Cisticola ☐
- Desert Cisticola ☐
- Pectorial-patch Cisticola ☐
- Rattling Cisticola ☐
- Red-faced Cisticola ☐
- Rock-loving Cisticola ☐
- Siffling Cisticola ☐
- Stout Cisticola ☐
- Trilling Cisticola ☐
- Winding Cisticola ☐
- Wing-snapping Cisticola ☐
- Zitting Cisticola ☐

Prinias   112

They can be recognised by cocked-up tails.

- Tawny-flanked Prinia ☐

Apalis   113

The Apalis occurs in all levels of forests and they feed on insects, usually caterpillars. The Apalis is a Warbler.

- Chestnut-throated Apalis ☐
- Grey-capped Apalis ☐
- Yellow-breasted Apalis ☐

Sylvietta/Crombec   114

They have very short tails and curved bills.

- Red-faced Sylvietta/Crombec ☐

Eremomelas   115

It is a Warbler with a short tail and yellow belly.

- Yellow-bellied Eremomela ☐

Parisomas   116

The Banded Parisoma is a warbler with a dark band on its chest.

- Brown Parisoma ☐
- Banded Parisoma ☐

Flycatchers   117

Pallid Flycatcher

Spotted Flycatcher

- African Dusky Flycatcher ☐
- Collared Flycatcher ☐
- Grey Flycatcher ☐
- Northern Black Flycatcher ☐
- Pallid Flycatcher ☐
- Spotted Flycatcher ☐
- Southern Black Flycatcher ☐
- Swamp Flycatcher ☐
- White-eyed Slaty Flycatcher ☐

Batis   118

It has a prominent chest band and yellow eyes.

- Chin-spot Batis ☐

Silverbird   119

Silverbird

- Silverbird ☐

The Silverbird is very common along the Seronera River. It is really a flycatcher with a distinct silver-grey back and tawny-orange underparts. It has a broad-based triangular bill. It is insectivorous, doing much of its feeding in the air.

Wattle-eyes   120

They can be recognised by the 'wattle' around their eyes.

- Banded Wattle-eye ☐
- Black-throated Wattle-eye ☐

Monarchs   121

- African Paradise Monarch ☐
- Blue Monarch ☐
- White-tailed Crested Monarch ☐

Paradise Monarch (female)

The Paradise Monarch male chases after the female, flaunting his long tail during courtship. The nest is a very neat, lichen-covered cup.

Paradise Monarch (male)

Bird check list

122 Babblers

African Hill-babbler ☐
Arrow-marked Babbler ☐
Black-lored Babbler ☐
Pied Babbler ☐

Arrow-marked Babbler

123 Chatterers

Rufous Chatterer ☐

124 Tits

Tits are very acrobatic and may hang upside down as they forage for insects and larvae on twigs.

African Penduline Tit ☐
Red-throated Tit ☐
White-bellied Black Tit ☐

125 White-eyes

Abyssinian White-eye ☐
Montaine White-eye ☐

They are monogamous, pair for life, non-territorial and gregarious. Pairs roost seperately. Can be recognised by white ring around eye.

Montaine White-eye

126 Sunbirds

Malachite Sunbird

Variable Sunbird

Amethyst Sunbird ☐
Beautiful Sunbird ☐
Bronze Sunbird ☐
Collared Sunbird ☐
Copper Sunbird ☐
Eastern Double-collared Sunbird ☐
Eastern Violet-backed Sunbird ☐
Golden-winged Sunbird ☐
Malachite Sunbird ☐
Marico Sunbird ☐

Sunbirds have long, curved bills with which they probe open blossoms or pierce the bases of tubular flowers to get to the nectaries. They have very long, tubular tongues which are split at the end for sipping the nectar.

Olive Sunbird ☐
Red-chested Sunbird ☐
Scarlet-chested Sunbird ☐
Scarlet-tufted Sunbird ☐
Variable Sunbird ☐

Orioles 127

African Black-headed Oriole ☐
African Golden Oriole ☐
Eurasian Oriole ☐

Orioles are known for their clear, liquid calls 'poodleeoo - poodleeoo'. They feed on caterpillars and other insects but will also eat berries.

Black-headed Oriole

Puffback Shrikes 128

The male fluffs white rump plumes during courtship

Black-backed Puffback Shrike ☐

Boubou Shrikes 129

The Boubou Shrikes usually occur in pairs and they call in a duet. They occur along streams or river edges.

Slate-coloured Boubou (Shrike) ☐
Tropical Boubou (Shrike) ☐

Brubru Shrikes 130

The Brubru prefers canopies of woodland.

Brubru (Shrike) ☐

Chagra Shrikes 131

Black-crowned Chagra

Black-crowned Chagra (Shrike) ☐
Brown-crowned Chagra (Shrike) ☐
Marsh Chagra (Shrike) ☐

Chagras are territorial, monogamous and they pair for life. They have elaborate courtship displays in which they spread their tail feathers to reveal the white outer ring.

Brown-crowned Chagra

Bird check list

132 Fiscal Shrikes

Common Fiscal ☐
Grey-backed Fiscal (Shrike) ☐
Long-tailed Fiscal (Shrike) ☐
Taita Fiscal (Shrike) ☐

Common Fiscal

Grey-backed Fiscal

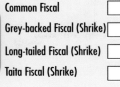

Taita Fiscal

133 Shrikes

Magpie Shrike

Black-fronted Bush-shrike ☐
Lesser Grey Shrike ☐
Magpie Shrike ☐
Red-backed Shrike ☐
Red-tailed Shrike ☐
Sulphur-breasted Bush-shrike ☐
White Helmet shrike ☐
Northern White-crowned Shrike ☐

Northern White-crowned Shrike

All Shrikes are predatory birds with hooked bills. They make a cup-shaped nest and often use cobwebs.

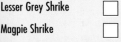
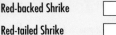

Red-backed Swike

134 Crows

Pied Crow

Pied Crow ☐

The crow is smaller than a raven, with a thinner bill, and larger than a Cape Rook. They usually scavenge and are often found near human habitation.

135 Rooks

Cape Rook/Black Crow ☐

The Cape Rook is smaller than the Pied Crow and less of a scavenger. They feed mainly on insects, frogs, fruits and grain. They tame well and make good pets.

Cape Rook

136 Ravens

White-naped Raven ☐

It can be recognised by a heavy bill and occurs from 400m to 4 000m above sea level and is therefore very widespread. It mainly scavenges.

White-naped Raven

137 Starlings

Greater Blue-eared Starling

Ashy Starling ☐
Greater Blue-eared Starling ☐
Hildebrandt's Starling ☐
Purple-headed Starling ☐
Red-winged Starling ☐
Rueppell's Long-tailed Starling ☐
Sharpe's Starling ☐
Superb Starling ☐
Violet-backed Starling ☐
Waller's Starling ☐
Wattled Starling ☐

Superb Starling

Wattled Starling

Red-winged Starlings stay together all year, so there is no need for courtship. Wattled starlings are nomadic, sociable and breed opportunistically when conditions are right. They build very large dome-shaped nests with a side entrance, much different to other starlings. The Red-winged starling nest colonially in 1-1,5 m deep holes in river banks.

Violet-backed Starling

BIRDS

138   Drongos

African Drongo ☐

Drongos are monogamous and aggressively territorial, chasing raptors relentlessly, even clinging to their backs and pecking them in flight. Their nests are placed hammock-like in the fork of a horizontal branch.

African Drongo

139   Oxpeckers

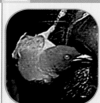

Red-billed Oxpecker ☐

Yellow-billed Oxpecker ☐

Oxpecker populations have declined since cattle dipping has deprived them of their staple diet - ticks. Their bills are flattened on the side, enabling them to shear the ticks from the animal's hide.

Red-billed Oxpecker

140   Sparrows

Grey-headed Sparrow ☐

Chestnut Sparrow ☐

Rufous Sparrow ☐

Sparrows are granivorous, ground-feeding birds of open country. They build untidy, domed nests with side entrances.

Malachite Sunbird

141   Weavers

Black-headed Weaver ☐

Black-necked Weaver ☐

Chestnut Weaver ☐

Grey-headed Social Weaver ☐

Grosbeak Weaver ☐

Grey-headed Social Weaver

Golden-backed Weaver ☐

Large Golden Weaver ☐

Lesser Masked Weaver ☐

Little Weaver ☐

Parasitic Weaver ☐

Lesser Masked Weaver

Red-billed Buffalo Weaver ☐

Red-headed Weaver ☐

Rufous-tailed Weaver ☐

Speckled Weaver ☐

Speckle-fronted Weaver ☐

Slender-billed Weaver ☐

Speke's Weaver ☐

Vitelline Masked Weaver ☐

White-headed Buffalo Weaver ☐

Red-billed Buffalo Weaver

Rufous-tailed Weaver

Most Weavers are parasitised by the Diederik Cuckoo.

Vitelline Masked Weaver

Red-headed Weaver

Speckled Weaver

White-headed Buffalo Weaver

Malimbas   142

This is a black bird with a red head.

Red-headed Malimba (Weaver) ☐

Widowbirds   143

Fan-tailed Widowbird ☐

Jackson's Widowbird ☐

Red-collared Widowbird ☐

White-winged Widowbird ☐

Females are short-tailed and dull.

Fan-tailed Widowbird

Bird check list

Male widowbirds develop prominent tails, they turn black and have coloured shoulders. After breeding they become dull, like the females. They have spherical, woven nests with side entrances. which are placed low in grass tufts or shrubs.

White-winged Widowbird

The Southern Cordon Bleu is also known as the Blue Waxbill. They breed in association with social wasps, but the reason is not certain. It has been suggested that wasps choose trees free of *Acacia* ants because the ants prey on their larvae. This association frees the birds of ants in the nest.

Southern Cordon Bleu

144 Bishops

Black Bishop	☐
Southern Red Bishop	☐
Yellow Bishop	☐
Yellow-crowned Bishop	☐

Southern Red Bishop

145 Queleas/Finches

Cardinal Quelea	☐
Red-billed Quelea	☐
Red-headed Quelea	☐

Queleas occur in flocks of millions and they feed on dry grass seeds, causing major damage to crops.

Red-billed Quelea

146 Whydahs

Breeding male wydahs develop long tail feathers. They are host-specific brood-parasites on Waxbills. They do not evict the host chicks and maintain a bond with the host parents for some time.

Acacia Paradise Whydah	☐
Straw-coloured Whydah	☐
Pin-tailed Whydah	☐
Steel-blue Whydah	☐

147 Blackfinches

Grey-crowned Blackfinch	☐

148 Cordon Bleus

Blue-capped Cordon Bleu	☐
Red-cheeked Cordon Bleu	☐
Southern Cordon Bleu	☐

Only the male of the Red-cheeked Cordon Bleu has red cheeks.

Red-cheeked Cordon Bleu

Crimsonwings 149

They occur in highland forest clearings.

Abyssinian Crimsonwing	☐

Cut-throat Finches 150

The male has a red band across the throat.

Cut-throat Finch	☐

Firefinches 151

African Firefinch	☐
Red-billed Firefinch	☐

They often occur on the ground and feed on grass seeds. Their colouration varies from red to maroon to brown.

Red-billed Firefinch

Grenadiers 152

Purple Grenadier	☐

Grenadiers are common in bush and are often on or near the ground. They feed on grass seeds. Their chicks have reflective tubercles at the side of the mouth indicating the position of the mouth in the dark nest. They have purple markings on the side of the head.

Purple Grenadier

Indigo Birds 153

They are parasitised by Firefinches

Village Indigobird	☐

Mannikins 154

The Bronze Mannikin builds a brooding nest in winter, separate from the breeding nest.

Bicoloured Mannikin	☐
Bronze Mannikin	☐

BIRDS

155 Oriole-finches

They have black heads and yellow bodies.

Oriole-finch ☐

156 Pytilias

Green-winged Pytilias ☐

Green-winged Pytilias

The Green-winged Pytilia is also known as the Melba Finch and is host to the Paradise Whydah. It finds most of its food (termites, seeds) on the ground. It favours areas of dense, low *Acacia* thickets, *A. tortilis* being a favourite.

157 Quailfinches

African Quailfinch ☐

158 Silverbills

They can be recognised by their grey heads and silver bills.

African Silverbill ☐

Grey-headed Silverbill ☐

159 Twinspots

Green Twinspot ☐

160 Waxbills

Waxbills have strong, conical bills suited to cracking and de-husking seeds. Food in the crops of birds is enriched by the addition of protein secretions before it is fed to the young. They are monogamous and mate for life. They reinforce the bond by mutual preening and huddling.

Black-cheeked Waxbill ☐

Black-faced Waxbill ☐

Common Waxbill ☐

Crimson-rumped Waxbill ☐

Fawn-breasted Waxbill ☐

Yellow-bellied Waxbill ☐

161 Buntings

Buntings can be distinguished from finches by their wavy-edged upper mandible.

Cinnamon-breasted Rock Bunting ☐

Golden-breasted Bunting ☐

Canaries 162

Yellow-fronted Canary

Yellow-crowned Canary ☐

Yellow-fronted Canary ☐

All canaries line their cup-shaped nests with downy plant material, usually white in colour. They are fine songsters and have regular song perches. Canary nests remain clean as faecal sacs are removed or eaten.

Citrils 163

African Citril ☐

Serins 164

Serins are closely related to canaries. The Grosbeak Serin has a thick bill.

Grosbeak Serin ☐

Streaky Serin ☐

Did You Know?

- The male Sandgrouse has specially adapted feathers that can absorb water, which is carried back to the chicks in the nest. The feathers have barbules that uncoil when they come into contact with water. These microscopic filaments soak up the water by capillary action. They can soak up to 22ml of water, of which about half or two thirds will make it to the nest. (Steyn, 1996).

- A flock of White Helmet-shrikes has a single breeding pair and all members assist in incubation, feeding the chicks and tending to sanitation of the nest. At sexual maturity, a group of brothers may team up with a group of sisters to form a new flock.

- Snake Eagles feed almost exclusively on snakes. The Brown Snake Eagle hunts from a perch and the Black-breasted Snake Eagle hunts on the wing. They both drop the snake to stun it and then sieze it again, swallowing it whole - head first. When they take snake prey to their chicks, they allow them to pull it out of their crop. The parent may assist the chick by pulling the snake out with its talons (claws). The chick can swallow up to a metre length at one time.

- Quelea Finches are the most abundant land birds in Africa. Their breeding is highly synchronised and is determined by protein levels in their blood. They will only breed if there is sufficient fresh grass seeds and larvae to feed their chicks. They have the shortest breeding cycle of all birds. Mating and nest-building takes ±10-12 days, even though they have to do ±700 round trips to collect material. They lay ±3 eggs over two days and each egg requires only ±30 hours for hatching. The young leave the nest at 11-13 days. The whole cycle may be only 35 days. The snake-like flocks that they form may represent about one million individuals and the continuus streams up to five million birds. They have a great economic impact on commercial crops.

BIRDS

CONTACT DETAILS

Contact details of safari companies, lodges and airline companies

Mobile Safari Companies

Bobby Camping Safaris
Tel: +255 27 254-4058
Reservations: +255 27 250- 7842
Fax: +255 27 254 4057
Mobile: +255 744-311-471 or
(0) 744-262-925
Fax: + 255 27 254-4058
E-mail: info@bobbycamping.com
or bobbycamping@habari.co.tz
Website:
www.bobbycamping.com

Bushbuck Safaris
Tel: +255 27 250-67779;
254-4186: 254- 4308; 254-8924
Fax: +255 27 254-4058
E-mail:
bushbuck@bushbuckltd.com
Website:
www.bobbycamping.com

Hoopoe Safaris
Tel: +255 27 250-7011
E-mail: information
@hoopoe.com
Website: www.hoopoe.com

Ker & Downey Safaris
Tel: +255 27 250-8917
Fax: + 255 27 250-8434
E-mail:
belinda.ambrose@tgts.com

Kudu Safaris Ltd
Tel: +255 27 250-6056
Fax: + 255 27 250-8108
E-mail: kudu@habari.co.tz

Leopard Tours
Tel: +255 27 250-3603
or +255 27 250-7906/8441/8443
Fax: + 255 27 250-8219/4131/4134
E-mail:
leopard@yako.habari.co.tz
Website: www.leopard-tours.com

Ranger Safaris
Tel: +255 27 250-3023/3074/3738
Fax: + 255 27 250-8205/8749
E-mail:
ranger@rangersafaris.co.tz
Website: www.rangersafaris.com

Roy Safaris
Tel: +255 27 250-8010/2115/7940
Fax: + 255 27 254-8892
E-mail: roysafaris@intafrica.com
Website: www.roysafaris.com

Unique Safaris
Tel: +255 27 255-3843/3863/3823
Fax: + 255 27 255-3858/3527
Mobile: +255 (0) 741-282-147
E-mail: uniquesaf@cybernet.co.tz
Website: uniquesafaris.com

Lodges in the area

CC Africa (CONSCORP LTD)
Tel: +255 27 254-8078/5849/
Fax: + 255 27 254-4058
Tel SA: +27 11 809-4300
Fax SA: +27 11 809-4400
E-mail: information @ccafrica.com
or arusha@ccafrica.co.tz
Website: www.ccafrica.com
LODGES: Klein's Camp (outside
Klein's Gate of Serengeti);
Grumeti River Camp (Kirawira
area in the Western Corridor of
Serengeti); Ngorongoro Crater
Lodge (Ngorongoro Crater rim);
Lake Manyara Tree Lodge (near
Lake Manyara National Park)

**Gibb's Farm (Ngorongoro
Safari Lodge)**
Tel: +255 27 253-4040
E-mail: bas.gibbs@habari.co.tz
Website:www.gibbsfarm.net
LODGES: Gibb's Farm (near
Karatu)

Kudu Lodge and Campsite
Tel: +255 27 253-4055/4268
Fax: +255 27 253-4268
Mobile: +255 744-474-792
E-mail:
kuducamp-lodge@kuducamp.com or
kuducamp@iwayafrica.com
Website: www.kuducamp.com
LODGES: Kudu Lodge and
Campsite (near Karatu)

Ndutu Safari Lodge
Tel: +255 27 250-8930/6702/2829;
253-7014
Tel Lodge: +255 27 253-7014/7015
Fax: + 255 27 250-8310
E-mailbookings:
bookings@ndutu.com
E-mail (other):
ndutugibbs@habari.co.tz or
ndutu@bushlink.co.tz
E-mail (lodge): info@ndutu.com
Website: www.ndutu.com
LODGES: Ndutu Lodge

(at Lake Ndutu)
Sanctuary Lodges
Tel: +255 27 250-9816/7
Fax: + 255 27 250-8237
E-mail:
tanzania@sanctuarylodges.com
Website:
www.sanctuarylodges.com
LODGES: Kusini Camp (± 40km
south-west of Lake Ndutu in south-
ern Serengeti); Swala Camp
(Tarangire National Park)

Serena Hotels
Tel: +255 22 250-8175
E-mail: rgomes@serena.co.tz
LODGES: Kirawira Serena
Tented Camp (Kirawira in the
western corridor of the Serengeti),
Serengeti Serena Lodge (near
Seronera in Serengeti), Ngorongoro
Serena Lodge (on the Ngorongoro
Crater rim).

CONTACT DETAILS

Serengeti Stop Over Ltd
Tel: +255 27 253-7095
Mobile: +255 748-422-359
E-mail:
info@serengetistopover.com
Website:
www.serengetistopover.com
LODGES: Serengeti Stop Over
Lodge (near Ndabaka Gate on the
Mwanza road).

Sopa Lodges & Elewana Africa
Tel: +255 27 250-0630
E-mail: info@sopalodges.com
Website: www.sopalodges.com or
www.elewana.com
LODGES: Serengeti Sopa Lodge
(near Moru Kopjes in the
Serengeti); Ngorongoro Sopa
Lodge (on the Ngorongoro Crater
rim)

Tarangire Safari Lodge
Tel: +255 27 254-4752 or
253-1447
Fax: +255 27 254-4752
Mobile: +255 (0) 748-202-777
E-mail: sss@habari.co.tz or
tarsaf@habari.co.tz
Website:
www.tarangiresafarilodge.com
LODGES: Tarangire Safari Lodge
(at Tarangire National Park)

Airline companies / Balloon Safaris

Air Excel Ltd
Tel: +255 27 250-1590/1595/7;
254-8429
Mobile: +255 (0) 741-510-857 or
(0)741-511- 227 or
(0) 744-211-227
E-mail:
reservations @airexcelonline.com

Air Tanzania Company Ltd
Tel: +255 27 250-3201
Fax: + 255 27 254-4058
E-mail:
airtanzania-ark@cybernet.co.tz
Website: www.airtanzania.com

Northern Air
Tel: +255 27 250-8059/60
E-mail:
northernair@habari.co.tz

Precision Air Services Ltd
Tel: +255 27 250-6903/2836/7319
E-mail:
information@precisionairtz.com
pwmarketing@precisionairtz.com
pwreservations@precisionairtz.com
Website: www.precisionairtz.com

Regional Air Services
Tel: +255 27 250-2541/4477/4164
E-mail:
sales@regional.co.tz
Website: www.regional.co.tz

Tanzanian Air Services (Tanzanair)
Tel: +255 22 284-3131/7319/7635
Fax: + 255 27 250-8204
E-mail:
information@precisionairtz.com
Website: www.precisionairtz.com

Serengti Balloon Safaris
Tel: +255 27 250-8578/8254/8967
or +255 748-422- 359
E-mail: balloons@habari.co.tz
Website: www.balloonsafaris.com
BASED: At Seronera in the
Serengeti National Park

Parks and Reserves / Government Organisations

Tanzania National Parks
Tel: +255 27 250-1930
Fax: +255 27 250-8216
E-mail: tanapa@yako.habari.co.tz
Website: www.tanapa.com
BASED: In Arusha

Ngorongoro Conservation Area
Tel: +255 27 250-3339 or
254-4625
Fax: +255 27 254-8752
E-mail: ncaa_faru@cybernet.co.tz
or ncaa_info@cybernet.co.tz
or ncaa-info@africaonline.co tz
Website:
www.ngorongoro-crater-africa.org
BASED: In Arusha and at the
Ngororongoro Crater

Tanzania Tourist Board (TTB)
Tel: +255 22 254-4754/5
E-mail:
sss@habari.co.tz or
tarsaf@habari.co.tz
Website:
www.tanzaniatouristboard.com

Car Hire

Fortes Car Hire
E-mail:
wendy@fortes-safaris.com
Website: www.fortescarhire.com

Avis Rent A Car
Tel. Dar-es-Salaam:
+255 22 211-5381
E-mail Dar-es-Salaam:
md@skylinktanzania.com
**Tel. Dar-es-Salaam International
Airport Branch:**
+255 22 284-2738

Tel. Arusha: +255 27 250-9108
Fax Arusha: +255 27 250-9109
E-mail Arusha:
skylink.arusha@cybernet.co.tz
Website:
www.skylinktanzania.com

The author does not take responsiblity for any changes in contact details

INDEX

Trees: **Bold names** are headings for groups such as Amphibaians, Animals, Birds, Trees, Wild Flowers etc.

4 - **Page numbers that are not bold or italic** indicate short references to a subject.

4 - **Bold page numbers** refer to a detailed description in the text to a subject.

4 - **Bold italic page numbers** refer to an identification picture of a certain plant, animal, reptile or bird.